MARLENA SPIELER

THE
CLASSIC
BARBECUE
AND
GRILL
COOKBOOK

MARLENA SPIELER
THE
CLASSIC
BARBECUE
AND
GRILL
COOKBOOK

DK

DORLING KINDERSLEY
LONDON • NEW YORK • SYDNEY • MOSCOW

A DORLING KINDERSLEY BOOK

Project Editor
Alexa Stace

Art Editor
Kate Scott

Assistant Designer
Emy Manby

Senior Editor
Carolyn Ryden

Senior Art Editor
Vanessa Courtier

Managing Editor
Susannah Marriott

Senior Managing Art Editor
Carole Ash

DTP Designer
Karen Ruane

Photography
Dave King

Production
Maryann Rogers
Manjit Sihra

First published in Great Britain in 1996
by Dorling Kindersley Limited,
9 Henrietta Street, London WC2E 8PS
Reprinted 1996
First published in paperback 1998

Copyright © 1996
Dorling Kindersley Limited, London
Text Copyright © 1996 Marlena Spieler

A CIP catalogue record for this book is available
from the British Library.

ISBN 0-7513-0569-3

Reproduced in Nottingham by Euroscan
Printed and bound in Spain by Artes Gráficas Toledo, S.A.
D.L. TO: 37-1999

CONTENTS

INTRODUCTION 6

CLASSIC DISHES 8

*A photographic introduction to ten
classic barbecue dishes and their ingredients*

MARINADES, RUBS & FLAVOURINGS 30

*A selection of piquant marinades, spicy dry
rubs and fragrant butters, oils and vinegars*

INTRODUCTION

The appeal of barbecuing is enormous. Before you even taste a morsel you will have been teased mercilessly by the delicious aromas that waft from the coals.

Barbecuing was the first cooking technique invented: early hunters would gather round a fire roasting hunks of freshly caught meat. Even today, with sophisticated barbecues and complex recipes, barbecuing remains essentially the same: cooking over fire.

Most of the happy occasions of my life have been accompanied by barbecues. My recent wedding feast, held in a Sonoma County vineyard, featured juicy Tuscan chicken cooked over an open fire, an array of summer vegetables and bowls of pungent aïoli. When my daughter celebrated her *batmitzvah*, we set up a huge barbecue and roasted a wide variety of delicacies for the party.

On travels, the meals I have most enjoyed have often been cooked over open fires. On a recent trip to France we ate a fireside feast of *cargolade* – snails and sausages, served with a garlicky sauce – in Perpignan. Near Cinque Terre I rigged up an impromptu barbecue on the beach and cooked the fish we had caught. One warm evening in a Languedoc café I nibbled merguez cooked over vine cuttings, a scruffy, albeit hopeful assortment of local dogs at my feet.

Whenever I've found myself snacking on street food, it has usually been cooked over hot coals. In Bulgaria, I have eaten roasted meat tucked into fat bread rolls along with crunchy salads, an Eastern European version of the *souvlakia* I have so often devoured in Greece. In Mexico, I have frequently been seduced by the promise of smoky-scented meat and fish wrapped up in a tortilla – and who could resist the scent of spicy roasting birds in Thailand?

Though fire-roasted foods are marvellous for entertaining, they do not need a special occasion; and though they are eaten all over the world, you do not need a passport to enjoy them. For delectable, memorable barbecuing and grilling, simply light the fire.

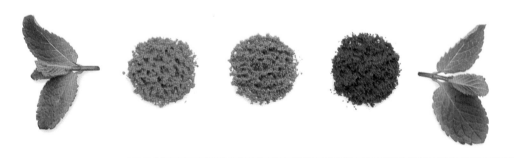

A few words about terminology: while barbecuing and grilling both take place over hot coals, there are some major differences. Cooking quickly over direct heat on an uncovered grill or barbecue is *grilling*: this results in meat, fish, poultry or vegetables that are succulent, the juices sealed in from the heat of the fire. Properly, the term *barbecuing* refers to long, slow cooking, covered, over smouldering hardwood. It is thought that the word derives from the Caribbean and Mexican term *barbacoa*, which describes the method of pit-cooking a whole goat, from the tip of its beard to the end of its tail. Traditionally, larger, fattier cuts of meat are barbecued, emerging from the fire permeated with smoky essence, crusty on the outside, well done yet tender and moist within.

I would like to dedicate this book to Gretchen Spieler, who although she may not realize it, taught me how to barbecue in her backyard.

CLASSIC DISHES

From a medley of kebabs that includes lamb brochettes, chicken tikka and curaçao-soaked fruits, to universal favourites such as juicy hamburgers, chargrilled vegetables and herb-scented fish, the following selection of dishes features foods that are most popularly cooked on barbecues the world over. Middle Eastern flavours dominate in a dish of cumin-encrusted lamb, while herb-scented Tuscan chicken evokes the Mediterranean. For added fire there are spicy Thai-style prawns and a Mexican feast of shredded beef and chicken fajitas, piled into floury tortillas and served with fiery salsas.

All recipes serve 4 unless otherwise stated.

CHARGRILLED VEGETABLES

A selection of seasonal vegetables, bathed in a garlicky marinade, then barbecued over hot coals, makes a lyrical feast. Tougher vegetables such as artichokes or potatoes need parboiling first, to soften them before they go on the barbecue.

INGREDIENTS

2 medium-sized artichokes, halved and
choke removed (see page 152)
4 garlic bulbs
8 large tomatoes, halved
2 fennel bulbs, halved or quartered
250g (8oz) asparagus, ends trimmed
4 spring onions, trimmed
2 courgettes, sliced lengthways
2 corn-on-the-cobs, cut into bite-sized lengths
8 baby pattypan squash, halved
3 peppers, green, red and yellow, cored, deseeded
and cut into thick strips or quarters
2–3 tbsp chopped mixed fresh herbs, such as basil,
parsley, oregano, rosemary, thyme, savory or marjoram
Garlic Marinade
175ml (6fl oz) olive oil
4 tbsp lemon juice or wine vinegar
salt and black pepper
4–6 garlic cloves, finely chopped
1–2 tbsp fresh chopped rosemary, or 1 tsp dried herbs,
such as herbes de Provence

PREPARATION

1 Parboil the artichokes for 8–10 minutes, then drain upside-down and place in a shallow dish.
2 Blanch the garlic bulbs in boiling water for 5–8 minutes, then drain.
3 To make the marinade, place the olive oil, lemon juice, salt and pepper, garlic and herbs in a bowl and mix well. Pour about 4 tablespoons of this marinade over the artichokes.
4 Place the vegetables in large bowls and divide the remaining marinade between them. Turn to coat and leave to marinate for 1½ hours.
5 Light the barbecue or preheat a gas barbecue.
6 Drain the vegetables, reserving the marinade. Cook the vegetables in batches over hot coals, turning them once, until just tender inside and chargrilled on the outside. Remove them to a platter as they are ready and sprinkle with the reserved marinade.
7 Serve sprinkled with the chopped fresh herbs, and accompanied by Bruschetta (see page 113) and Red Chilli Aïoli (see page 124).

Mixed fresh herbs

Green, red and yellow peppers

Pattypan squash

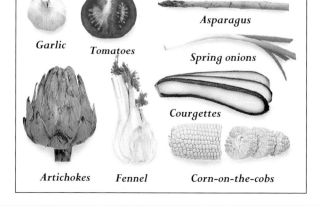

Garlic   *Tomatoes*   *Asparagus*   *Spring onions*   *Courgettes*   *Artichokes*   *Fennel*   *Corn-on-the-cobs*

Salt

Black
pepper

Garlic

Rosemary

Lemon juice

Olive oil

MEDITERRANEAN FISH

These barbecued fish remind me of the first time I went to Italy: we arrived in a little fishing village on the northeast coast and immediately stopped at the market for provisions. A cache of small fish went into my bag, along with fennel, peppers, garlic and parsley. We rigged up a primitive barbecue on the beach and cooked the fish, serving them with a salad of fennel and red peppers, and with chunks of bread to scoop it all up.

INGREDIENTS

1kg (2lb) sardines, sprats or whitebait,
with heads still on, cleaned only if they are
larger than 10–12 cm (4–5in)
3 garlic cloves, finely chopped
juice of ½ lemon
2 tbsp Pernod, Ouzo or
other anise-flavoured alcohol
3 tbsp olive oil
2 tbsp chopped fresh parsley
salt and black pepper
lemon wedges, to garnish

PREPARATION

1 Place the fish in a large shallow dish and add the garlic, lemon juice, Pernod, olive oil and half the parsley. Turn to coat well, then leave for 30–60 minutes at room temperature.
2 Light the barbecue or preheat a gas barbecue.
3 Drain the fish and cook over hot coals for approximately 3–4 minutes on each side, until they develop grill marks and are just cooked through. If cooked covered, they may not need turning.
4 Season well, then serve immediately, garnished with wedges of lemon and sprinkled with the remaining parsley. Accompany with a salad of fennel and peppers.

VARIATIONS

SNAPPER, BASS OR TILAPIA Larger fish, about 1–1.5kg (2–3lb), can also be cooked very successfully in this way. Cut 2–3 deep diagonal slashes on both sides of the fish, so that the marinade flavours can permeate the flesh. Cook for 10–20 minutes on each side, until cooked through, using a wire basket if possible.
GRILLED FISH WITH MOROCCAN FLAVOURS Omit the Pernod and double the amount of lemon juice. Substitute fresh coriander for half the parsley and add a large pinch each of curry powder, ground cumin and turmeric to the marinade.

Olive oil

Lemon juice

Pernod

Garlic

Sardines

Parsley

Salt

Black
pepper

Lemon wedges

GRILLED SALMON WITH LEEKS

S almon is an ideal fish to barbecue. Its slightly oily texture holds
up well to the heat of the fire, and its distinctive flavour
combines well with the smoky scent of the barbecue. The
lemony chive and watercress butter makes a tangy fresh sauce
as it melts on to the fish. Chargrilled baby leeks are a
marvellous accompaniment; if they are unavailable, use
ordinary-sized leeks, or raw spring onions tossed with
olive oil and vinegar before barbecuing.

Butter

Black pepper

Salt

Olive oil

Salmon steaks

Baby leeks

INGREDIENTS

8 baby leeks, cleaned and trimmed
4 x 2.5cm (1in) thick salmon steaks,
about 250g (8oz) each
3 tbsp olive oil or melted butter
salt and black pepper
Chive, Lemon & Watercress Butter
60g (2oz) butter, softened
1 garlic clove, finely chopped
1 shallot, finely chopped
2 tbsp chopped chives
45g (1½ oz) watercress, chopped
juice of ½ lemon
salt and black pepper

PREPARATION

1 Light the barbecue or preheat a gas barbecue.
2 Meanwhile, make the flavoured butter.
Combine the butter with the garlic, shallot, chives
and watercress, then blend in the lemon juice and
seasoning. Drain off any excess liquid and form the
butter into a sausage shape. Wrap in clingfilm and
chill until firm.
3 Blanch the leeks in boiling water for about 2
minutes, then drain, refresh under cold running
water and drain well again.
4 Brush the salmon and the leeks with oil or
melted butter. Sprinkle with salt and pepper.
5 Place the fish and leeks on the barbecue over
medium-hot coals and cook for 3–5 minutes on
each side, until the salmon is fairly firm and the
leeks have char marks from the grill.
6 Serve immediately, with a nugget of the chilled
butter on top of each salmon steak.

VARIATION

GRILLED STEAKS WITH LEEKS Tender lean steaks
are delicious with the melting Chive, Lemon &
Watercress Butter. Adjust the cooking time to 4–5
minutes so that the meat remains rare and juicy.

Garlic

Shallot

Chives

Watercress

Lemon juice

THAI-STYLE PRAWNS

A hot, spicy marinade and coconut-flavoured sauce give these prawns the authentic flavour of Thailand. Serve with Southeast Asian Noodle Salad (see page 134) or crisp raw bean-sprouts. Halve the quantity of marinade if serving prawns as a starter.

INGREDIENTS

*raw tiger prawns in their shells,
heads removed, 12 for starters or
24 for a main dish
walnut-sized piece of creamed coconut
blended with 4 tbsp water, or
4 tbsp unsweetened coconut milk
chilli flowers (see page 153), to garnish*

Thai Marinade

*¼ red pepper, cored, deseeded
and finely chopped
4 garlic cloves, finely chopped
2 tbsp chopped fresh coriander
2 tbsp vinegar
juice of 2 limes
1 stalk lemongrass, finely chopped,
or rind of ¼ lemon
½ tsp turmeric, or to taste
4 tbsp vegetable oil
pinch of ground cumin
1–2 green chillies, finely chopped
½ tsp crushed dried red chillies,
or red chilli paste
1 tsp sugar, or to taste*

PREPARATION

1 Light the barbecue or preheat a gas barbecue.
2 Combine the marinade ingredients in a bowl. Place the tiger prawns in a shallow dish and pour over the marinade. Turn until well coated, then refrigerate for 30 minutes.
3 Get 4 or 8 skewers ready – wooden skewers should be soaked in cold water for 30 minutes.
4 Drain the prawns, reserving the marinade. Thread 3 or 4 prawns on each skewer, piercing each prawn twice. Cook over medium-hot to hot coals, about 2–3 minutes on each side, basting once or twice, until the prawns are pink.
5 Meanwhile, pour the marinade into a small pan, stir in the coconut milk and heat over the barbecue until the sauce thickens, about 5 minutes.
6 To serve, arrange some Southeast Asian Noodle Salad (see page 134) on each plate with the prawns on skewers. Pour over the hot sauce, and garnish with a chilli flower (see page 153).

Lemongrass

Lime juice

Coriander

Vinegar

Garlic

Red pepper

Creamed coconut

Tiger prawns

Turmeric

Vegetable oil

Cumin

Green
chillies

Crushed red
chillies

Sugar

Chilli
flower

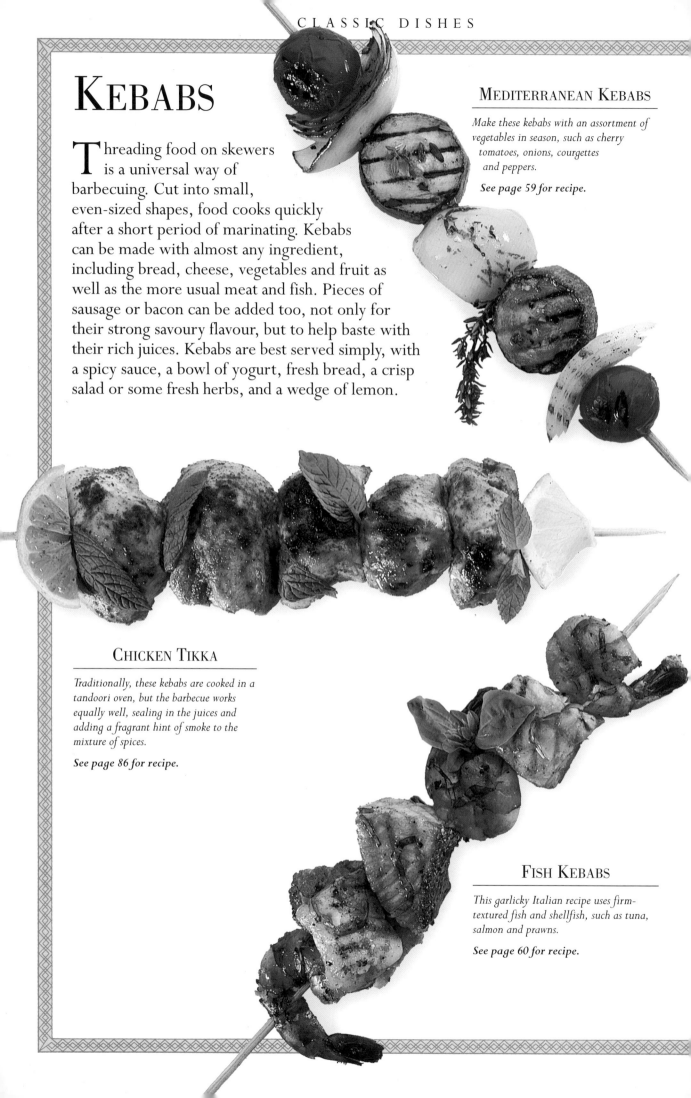

KEBABS

Threading food on skewers is a universal way of barbecuing. Cut into small, even-sized shapes, food cooks quickly after a short period of marinating. Kebabs can be made with almost any ingredient, including bread, cheese, vegetables and fruit as well as the more usual meat and fish. Pieces of sausage or bacon can be added too, not only for their strong savoury flavour, but to help baste with their rich juices. Kebabs are best served simply, with a spicy sauce, a bowl of yogurt, fresh bread, a crisp salad or some fresh herbs, and a wedge of lemon.

MEDITERRANEAN KEBABS

Make these kebabs with an assortment of vegetables in season, such as cherry tomatoes, onions, courgettes and peppers.

See page 59 for recipe.

CHICKEN TIKKA

Traditionally, these kebabs are cooked in a tandoori oven, but the barbecue works equally well, sealing in the juices and adding a fragrant hint of smoke to the mixture of spices.

See page 86 for recipe.

FISH KEBABS

This garlicky Italian recipe uses firm-textured fish and shellfish, such as tuna, salmon and prawns.

See page 60 for recipe.

HALLOUMI, TOMATO & BAY LEAF KEBABS

Serve these kebabs with crusty bread for an ideal snack or on their own as a wonderful appetizer.

See page 119 for recipe.

CURAÇAO FRUIT KEBABS

Almost any fruit can be cooked on the barbecue. These peach, banana and apricot kebabs are hot and smoky, yet sweet. Serve with a bowl of vanilla ice-cream.

See page 122 for recipe.

MOROCCAN LAMB BROCHETTES

Serve these brochettes hot off the grill, sprinkled with paprika and freshly chopped coriander.

See page 98 for recipe.

TUSCAN CHICKEN

A marinade of olive oil and lemon juice, combined with garlic and sprigs of fresh rosemary, is perfect for flavouring chicken to produce a classic Tuscan taste. I like to add a selection of vegetables – here peppers, courgettes and asparagus – but you can use whatever is in season. Good quality herbed chicken sausages would also make an enticing addition to the feast. Serve the chicken with Aïoli (see page 66) and a sprinkling of black olives.

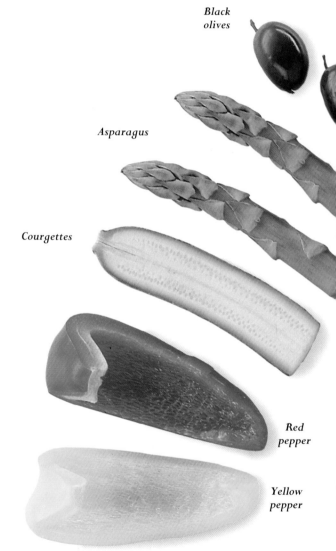

Black olives

Asparagus

Courgettes

Red pepper

Yellow pepper

INGREDIENTS

1 chicken, about 1.5kg (3lb), jointed into 8 pieces
1 yellow and 1 red pepper, cored,
deseeded and cut into wedges
4 small courgettes, sliced lengthways
500g (1lb) asparagus, ends trimmed
handful of black olives, to garnish
Tuscan Marinade
10 garlic cloves, finely chopped
juice of 3 lemons
2–3 tbsp chopped fresh rosemary
salt and black pepper
90ml (3fl oz) olive oil

PREPARATION

1 To make the marinade, combine the garlic, lemon juice, rosemary, a good pinch of salt, some black pepper and the olive oil in a small bowl and blend well.
2 Place the chicken pieces in a large shallow dish. Pour two-thirds of the marinade over the chicken, reserving the remainder to baste the vegetables. Cover the chicken and refrigerate for at least 2 hours (overnight, or even for 2 nights, is ideal).
3 Light the barbecue or preheat a gas barbecue.
4 When the coals are medium-hot, arrange the chicken on the grill, adding dark meat first and breast meat last. Move the pieces around so that they cook evenly. If the barbecue has a lid, cover and cook the chicken pieces over indirect heat.
5 When the chicken is almost done (approximately 8–10 minutes for white meat and 20 minutes for dark meat, or until the juices run clear when the flesh is pierced with a skewer), toss the peppers, courgettes and asparagus in half the remaining marinade. Place the vegetables on the grill and cook for about 2 minutes on each side, basting them with the rest of the marinade.
6 To serve, pile the vegetables around the chicken pieces. Garnish with black olives and serve accompanied by Aïoli (see page 66).

Chicken

Garlic

Lemon
juice

Rosemary

Salt

Black
pepper

Olive oil

CUMIN ROAST LAMB

Cumin paste gives a rustic, Middle Eastern scent to food – try it also with fish fillets or steaks, such as snapper, cod or halibut. To serve this dish, I like to pile the grilled meat and vegetables around a central platter of Pilaff (see page 133) to create a communal feast. Leave the pumpkin unpeeled: the skin helps it keep its shape and is easily removed after cooking.

Olive oil

Aubergine

Pumpkin

INGREDIENTS

4 baby leeks or small brown onions, or 8 spring onions
500g (1lb) pumpkin or other orange winter squash,
cut into 5mm (¼in) slices, unpeeled
1 aubergine, cut into wedges or thick slices
2 tbsp olive oil
juice of ½ lemon
4 lamb steaks, about 175–250g (6–8oz) each
coriander leaves, to garnish
Cumin Paste
2 tbsp cumin seeds
2 tbsp ground cumin
6 garlic cloves, crushed
1 tsp salt
4 tbsp olive oil
2 tbsp chopped fresh coriander or parsley
juice of 1 lemon

PREPARATION

1 Place the cumin paste ingredients in a bowl and mix well together.
2 Blanch the leeks for 1–2 minutes in boiling water, then drain well. Place in a shallow dish with the pumpkin and aubergine.
3 Drizzle the vegetables with the olive oil and lemon juice, then scatter on 1–2 tablespoons of the cumin paste and turn to coat well.
4 Place the lamb steaks in a shallow dish and sprinkle on the remaining cumin paste, turning to coat well on all sides. Leave the lamb and vegetables to marinate for at least 30 minutes.
5 Meanwhile, light the barbecue or preheat a gas barbecue.
6 Place the meat and vegetables on the barbecue over hot coals. Turn everything once or twice while cooking, so that the lamb is browned on the outside but still pink inside, and the vegetables are tender, with grill marks.
7 Serve the lamb and vegetables with Middle Eastern Spiced Pilaff (see page 133) and garnish with coriander leaves. Accompany with Cucumber-yogurt Relish (see page 129), if liked.

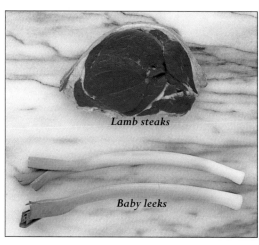

Lamb steaks

Baby leeks

Lemon juice

Cumin
seeds

Ground
cumin

Garlic

Salt

Coriander

ALL-AMERICAN RIBS

Barbecued ribs are traditionally rubbed with a dry spice mixture, then basted, or "mopped", as they cook on the barbecue. The secret of their flavour is long slow cooking, the ribs growing tender and smoky as they cook on the fire. Brush the sweet and spicy She-devil Barbecue Sauce (see page 127) on the ribs during the last 10 minutes of cooking, and offer an extra bowlful at the table.

Garlic granules

INGREDIENTS

1kg (2lb) pork spare ribs, either
in a sheet or separated
4 leeks, cut into brushes
(see page 152), for basting
Down-home Dry Rub
1 tbsp onion granules
1 tbsp salt
1 tsp black pepper
3 tbsp paprika
1 tbsp dry mustard
1 tbsp garlic granules
1 tbsp crumbled dried bay leaves
Lone Star Moppin' Sauce
150ml (¼ pint) cider vinegar
90ml (3fl oz) vegetable oil
60ml (4 tbsp) Worcestershire sauce
½ tsp Tabasco
1 tbsp paprika
1 tbsp mild chilli powder
1 tsp dry mustard
1 tsp crumbled dried bay leaves
1 tsp garlic granules
½ tsp celery salt, or to taste

Dry mustard

Paprika

Black pepper

Salt

PREPARATION

1 Mix the dry rub ingredients together in a bowl. Dust the ribs with the dry rub, then rub it in well. Leave to marinate for 30 minutes.
2 Light the barbecue or preheat a gas barbecue.
3 To make the Lone Star Moppin' Sauce, place all the ingredients in a bowl and mix well together.
4 Cook the ribs on a cool part of the grill, basting with the Moppin' Sauce, using a leek brush. Keep covered, so that the smoke scents the meat. The longer and slower the ribs cook, the more tender they will be. Allow 1–2 hours if the ribs are in a sheet; about 40 minutes if separated. To cook over medium heat, halve the cooking time.
5 Brush with She-devil Barbecue Sauce (see page 127) when the ribs are almost done. Serve immediately, offering round the remaining sauce.

Onion granules

Pork spare ribs

Vegetable oil

Tabasco

Bay leaves

Cider vinegar

Worcestershire
sauce

Mild chilli
powder

Celery salt

FAJITAS

A Mexican feast, fajitas consist of various kinds of meat, such as chicken, beef and sometimes sausage, marinated in a spicy chilli paste then barbecued with plantains and onions until crusty and smoky-flavoured. Traditionally, the meats are then shredded and served in flour tortillas or crisp corn tacos with an accompaniment of guacamole, refried beans, sour cream and salsa. The contrast between the smoky meats, spicy salsa, soft tortillas, earthy beans and tangy cream is superb. See page 99 for the Fajitas recipe.

SHREDDED BEEF

Thinly sliced or shredded beef is perfect for tortilla fillings. **See page 99 for recipe.**

SALSA

Quick to prepare, salsa can be puréed for a smoother texture. **See page 124 for recipe.**

SOUR CREAM

Serve this tangy cream sprinkled with paprika, as a cooling accompaniment to spicy dishes.

REFRIED BEANS

Spicy puréed pinto beans. **See page 132 for recipe.**

GUACAMOLE

Avocado dip is one of the traditional side dishes. **See page 126 for recipe.**

PLANTAINS & ONIONS

Barbecued onions and slices of plantain make a superb contrast in flavour.
See page 99 for recipe.

FAJITAS

Traditionally, fajitas are served in a flour tortilla.
See page 99 for recipe.

SHREDDED CHICKEN

Chicken is first spread with chilli and tequila paste.
See page 99 for recipe.

BURGERS

What springs to mind when you think of a burger is a juicy meat patty, cooked over a charcoal fire, stuffed into a plump bun and slathered with piquant relishes. This sandwich got its name at the turn of the century, when sailors from Hamburg, Germany, docked in New York. Snacking on charcoal-grilled burgers sold from street stalls, some sailors had the idea of tucking them into bread rolls to carry back to their ship. The public first encountered this sandwich at the Louisiana Purchase Exposition in 1903–4 in St Louis, and it became an instant classic.

Salt

INGREDIENTS

750g (1½lb) lean minced beef
8 shallots or 1 onion, finely chopped
3–4 tbsp double cream or
extra-thick single cream
4 small flat ice cubes
salt and black pepper
4 sesame buns
sliced tomato, onion and pickled gherkins, to garnish
Shredded Lettuce Burger Sauce
125g (4oz) mayonnaise
3 tbsp French mustard, or a combination of
brown and American yellow mustard
½ iceberg lettuce or 1 whole
green lettuce, shredded
4 shallots, finely chopped
juice of ½ lemon

Ice cubes

Double cream

Shallots

PREPARATION

1 Light the barbecue or preheat a gas barbecue.
2 Place the beef in a large bowl and break it up with a fork. Add the shallots and cream and beat with a wooden spoon until well combined.
3 Using wet hands, shape the mixture into 4 large balls, then flatten with your fingers into patties about 2.5cm (1in) thick. Insert a small ice cube in the centre of each patty to keep the meat moist.
4 Generously sprinkle the patties with salt and pepper and place on the barbecue over hot coals. Cook for 3 minutes, then turn to cook the other side. Continue until the meat is done to taste.
5 To make the sauce, blend the mayonnaise and mustard together in a bowl. Add the lettuce and shallots and toss until well combined. Season with lemon juice to taste.
6 Split the sesame buns and toast on the barbecue. Serve each burger in a bun, topped with the sauce. Garnish with sliced tomato, onion rings and pickled gherkins.

Minced beef

Sesame buns

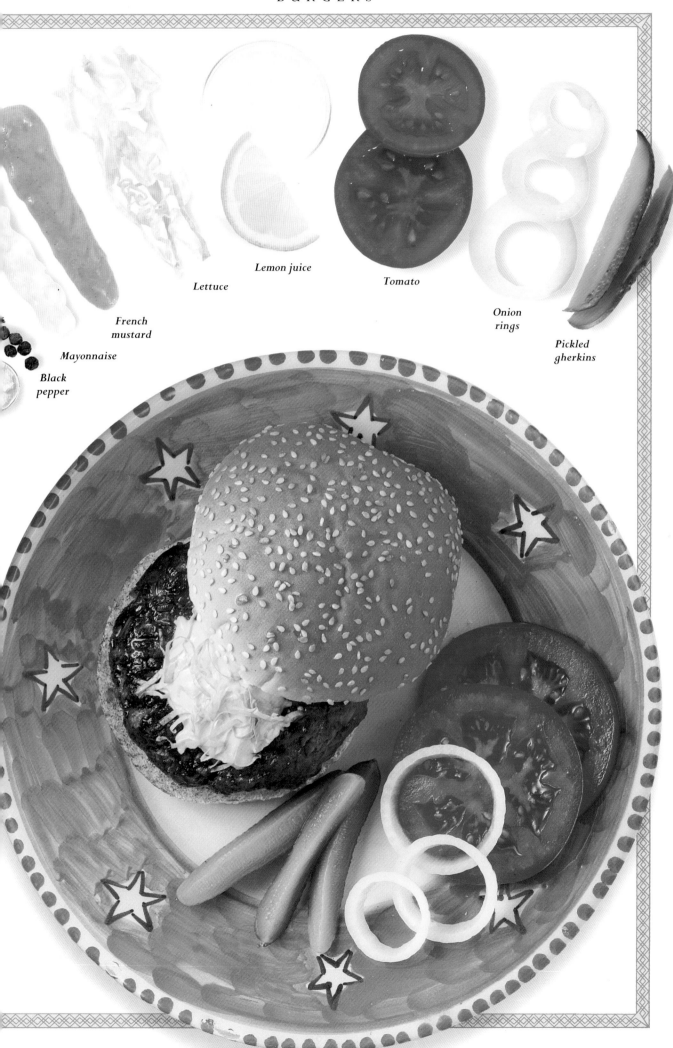

French
mustard

Mayonnaise

Black
pepper

Lettuce

Lemon juice

Tomato

Onion
rings

Pickled
gherkins

MARINADES, RUBS & FLAVOURINGS

*Bathing food in an aromatic marinade helps
to tenderize and add succulence while protecting
it from the heat of the fire. Hot spices, pungent
sauces and zesty citrus juices all imbue foods with
distinct tastes. Some marinades form glazes, while dry
rubs add piquancy. To add character to marinades,
steep your favourite herbs and spices in oils and
vinegars. Serve flavoured butters on top of
the cooked food for an extra smooth, rich finish.*

MARINADES

A simple marinade can transform food for the barbecue, whether meat, fish, poultry or vegetables. Not only does it enhance the flavour, but it helps to prevent moisture loss. Acidic marinades containing wine, vinegar, mustard or citrus juice penetrate and tenderize food. Oil and paste marinades form a savoury crust that seals in moisture, while dry herb and spice marinades are rubbed into food just before cooking.

TIMING & PREPARATION

♦ Red meat, poultry and game (whole and jointed) are usually marinated for up to 2 hours at room temperature or up to 48 hours in the refrigerator.
♦ Whole fish, fillets and steaks and seafood can be marinated for up to 30 minutes at room temperature, or up to 2 hours in the refrigerator.
♦ Vegetables and tofu can be marinated for up to 30 minutes at room temperature, or up to 2 hours in the refrigerator — overnight for tofu.
  ♦ Bring refrigerated food back to room temperature before cooking, and brush off excess marinade.

Garlic

Chilli paste

Paprika

Ground cumin

Oregano

Beer

SPICY MEXICAN MARINADE

This spicy marinade gives a rich red coating. Sufficient for 1kg (2lb) lean meat or fish.

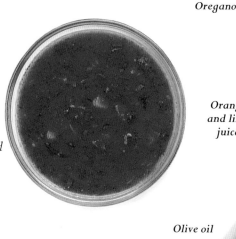

Orange and lime juice

INGREDIENTS

3 garlic cloves, finely chopped
1 tbsp chilli powder, lightly toasted and mixed to a paste with water
1 tbsp paprika
1 tsp ground cumin
½ tsp dried oregano
2 tbsp beer or tequila
juice of 1 orange and 1 lime, or
3 tbsp pineapple juice
2 tbsp olive oil
2 tbsp chopped fresh coriander
coarsely ground salt, to taste

Olive oil

Coriander

Salt

PREPARATION

Combine the ingredients in a shallow dish. Add the food, turn to coat and leave to marinate (see above for timing).

Rosemary Fennel Black Salt
seeds pepper

Sage

Oregano

Parsley

Olive oil

Lemon and
juice

Garlic

LEMON-HERB MARINADE

*Sufficient for 1kg (2lb) chicken, pork
or fish, or 750g (1½lb) vegetables.*

INGREDIENTS

*3 garlic cloves, finely chopped
1 lemon, thinly sliced
juice of 1 lemon
3 tbsp olive oil
30g (1oz) mixed fresh parsley, oregano, sage
and rosemary, finely chopped
1 tsp fennel seeds
black pepper and coarsely ground salt, to taste*

PREPARATION

Combine the ingredients in a dish. Add the
food and leave (see page 32 for timing).

SOUTH SEAS COCONUT MARINADE

*This marinade is finished off with an apricot glaze.
Enough to marinate 500g (1lb) fish fillets.*

INGREDIENTS

1 tbsp curry powder
1 tbsp soy sauce or fish sauce
125ml (4fl oz) coconut milk
juice of 1 lime
2 tbsp apricot jam or chutney
cayenne pepper, to taste

PREPARATION

1 Combine the curry powder, soy sauce, coconut milk and half the lime juice. Pour over the fish and leave to marinate (see page 32 for timing).
2 Mix the remaining lime juice with the jam and cayenne pepper. Brush the fish with this glaze during the last few minutes of cooking.

AFRO-CAJUN MARINADE

For crisp, spicy chicken wings; enough for 1kg (2lb).

INGREDIENTS

juice of 2–3 lemons
1 onion, grated
6 garlic cloves, finely chopped
½ tsp ground cumin
1 tbsp syrup from a jar of preserved ginger
¼ tsp ground cinnamon
pinch of ground cloves
¼ tsp cayenne pepper, or to taste
1 tbsp vegetable or olive oil

PREPARATION

Combine the ingredients in a dish, toss the chicken to coat well and leave (see page 32 for timing).

SWEET-SPICY MUSTARD MARINADE

*Marvellous for tiny kebabs, chicken wings, prawns
or lamb chops. Enough to coat 750g (1½lb).*

INGREDIENTS

60g (2oz) apricot jam or marmalade
1 tbsp Dijon mustard
30g (1oz) honey
1 tbsp brown sugar
1 tbsp cider vinegar
1 tbsp sesame oil

PREPARATION

Combine the ingredients in a shallow dish, toss the food to coat well and cook quickly over a high heat – the sugar will char with long cooking.

GREEN MASALA MARINADE

Perfect for lamb chops or cutlets; enough to coat 1kg (2lb).

INGREDIENTS

1 bulb garlic, cloves separated and finely chopped
3 tbsp lemon juice
3 tbsp natural yogurt
1 tsp ground cumin
1 tsp turmeric
1 tsp ground coriander
1 tsp garam masala
15g (½oz) fresh mint leaves, finely chopped
15g (½oz) fresh coriander leaves, finely chopped
5 cardamom pods, hulls removed and seeds crushed
150ml (¼ pint) olive oil
salt and cayenne pepper, to taste

PREPARATION

Mix the marinade in a shallow dish, add the meat and marinate (see page 32 for timing).

Afro-Cajun Marinade

Green Masala Marinade

TIKKA MASALA MARINADE

Ideal for giving an authentic, spicy Indian flavour to bland foods such as tofu or chicken pieces. Enough for 1kg (2lb) chicken pieces or 1 cake of tofu.

INGREDIENTS

2 garlic cloves, finely chopped
1 tsp chopped ginger root
2 tbsp natural yogurt
pinch of cayenne pepper
2-3 tsp cumin seeds
pinch of turmeric
1 tbsp tandoori or tikka paste
2 tbsp chopped fresh coriander

PREPARATION

Combine the ingredients well in a shallow dish. Add the tofu or chicken and turn to coat well. Leave to marinate (see page 32 for timing).

TERIYAKI MARINADE

This Japanese-style marinade is enough to coat 1kg (2lb) fish, poultry or meat.

INGREDIENTS

4 tbsp soy sauce
4 tbsp sesame oil
4 tbsp rice wine or dry sherry
2 tbsp sugar
2 spring onions, thinly sliced
2 garlic cloves, chopped
1 tsp grated ginger root

PREPARATION

Combine the ingredients in a shallow dish, add the food, turn to coat well and leave to marinate (see page 32 for timing).

HOISIN MARINADE

A classic Chinese sauce; enough for 750g (1½lb) chops.

INGREDIENTS

250ml (8fl oz) hoisin sauce
2–3 tbsp rice vinegar
2 tbsp soy sauce
5 garlic cloves, finely chopped
pinch of five-spice powder
1 tbsp sugar
2 tbsp sesame oil
dash of Tabasco

PREPARATION

Combine the ingredients, turn the chops to coat well and leave to marinate (see page 32 for timing).

BASIC YOGURT MARINADE

Suitable for 1kg (2lb) chicken, lamb or fish.

INGREDIENTS

250g (8oz) plain yogurt
2–3 garlic cloves, finely chopped
1 onion, finely chopped or grated
½ tsp ground cinnamon
½ tsp ground cumin
½ tsp crushed black peppercorns
¼ tsp ground ginger
¼ tsp cloves
¼ tsp nutmeg
¼ tsp cayenne pepper
2 cardamom pods, hulls removed and seeds crushed
1 tsp salt

PREPARATION

Combine well, add the food and leave to marinate (see page 32 for timing).

Teriyaki Marinade

Basic Yogurt Marinade

Garlic

Spring onions

Molasses sugar

Lemon zest and juice

Chillies

Soy sauce

Turmeric

Ground coriander

Ginger root

Peanuts

INDONESIAN MARINADE

Enough for 4 small poussins or 1.75kg (3½lb) chicken pieces.

INGREDIENTS

5–7 garlic cloves, finely chopped
4 spring onions or 5 shallots, chopped
4 tbsp molasses sugar
grated zest and juice of 2 lemons
2–3 green Jalapeño chillies,
finely chopped
90ml (3fl oz) soy sauce
½ tsp turmeric
1 tbsp ground coriander
3 tbsp finely chopped ginger root
100g (3½oz) peanuts, ground or finely chopped

PREPARATION

Mix the ingredients in a shallow dish. Add the chicken pieces, turn to coat well and leave for 3–4 hours at room temperature, or up to 48 hours in the refrigerator.

Bay
leaves

Herbes de
Provence

Salt

Black
pepper

Garlic

Onions

Sugar

Red wine

Pomegranate
syrup

INGREDIENTS

125ml (4fl oz) pomegranate syrup (grenadine)
4 tbsp red wine
2 tbsp sugar
2 onions, grated
5 garlic cloves, coarsely chopped
5–8 fresh bay leaves
2 tsp herbes de Provence
salt and black pepper

POMEGRANATE & WINE MARINADE

*This tangy-sweet marinade is ideal for rich lamb or
duck flesh. It is enough for 2 medium-sized ducks
cut into serving pieces, or 1kg (2lb) lamb chops.*

PREPARATION

Combine the ingredients in a large shallow dish.
Add the duck or lamb chops, and turn to coat well.
Cover and leave to marinate for 3–4 hours at room
temperature, or up to 48 hours in the refrigerator.

Olive oil

Red wine

Shallots

Garlic

Fresh herbs

Salt

Black pepper

BASIC WINE MARINADE

This basic marinade can be varied to taste. In general, red meat such as beef, duck or lamb will require a red wine marinade, chicken and fish a white one, but I have marinated chicken breasts in red wine with marvellous results. Makes enough for 1kg (2lb) meat, poultry or fish.

INGREDIENTS
4 tbsp olive oil
4 tbsp red or white wine
2 shallots, finely chopped or 1 onion, grated
2 garlic cloves, finely chopped, optional
1 tbsp chopped fresh herbs
salt and black pepper

PREPARATION
Combine the ingredients in a shallow dish. Add meat or fish of choice, turn to coat well and leave to marinate (see page 32 for timing).

Black
pepper

Ginger
root

Ground
allspice

Thyme

Onions

Chillies

Garlic

Tarragon
vinegar

Soy sauce

White wine

INGREDIENTS

4 tbsp white or red wine
2 tbsp tarragon vinegar
2 tbsp soy sauce
5–8 garlic cloves, finely chopped
1–2 Scots bonnet chillies, finely chopped
2 onions, finely chopped
1 tsp black pepper
1 tbsp finely chopped ginger root
1 tsp ground allspice
1 tsp dried thyme

JAMAICAN JERK

Throughout Jamaica "jerk" seasoning is used for marinating meats that are then roasted over the open fire until brown, crusty and spicy hot. Makes enough to marinate 1kg (2lb) beef, pork or chicken.

PREPARATION

Combine the ingredients in a shallow dish and toss the meat in the mixture to coat well. Leave to marinate (see page 32 for timing).

DRY RUBS

Dry rubs are mixtures of spices and herbs that are rubbed into food before cooking. They have no oil to moisten or acids to tenderize; they are all flavour. Use with fatty cuts of meat, or mix with a little oil and wine for a flavouring paste to brush on before grilling. Dry rubs are also good used with basting sauces, such as She-devil Barbecue Sauce (see page 127). The spice-herb coating gives a lovely crispness to the food and the sauce finishes it off.

CAJUN SPICE RUB

Makes enough for 1kg (2lb) meat.

INGREDIENTS

2 tbsp paprika
1 tbsp ground cumin
1 tbsp dried thyme
1 tbsp onion granules
1 tbsp garlic granules
1 tbsp dried oregano
1 tsp black pepper
1 tsp cayenne pepper

PREPARATION

Rub on food to be barbecued quickly and simply. Serve with a flavoured butter (see pages 42–43).

Paprika

Ground cumin

Thyme

Onion granules

Garlic granules

Oregano

Black pepper

Cayenne pepper

PASTES & GLAZES

Aromatic spicy pastes give a great flavour to any barbecued food. Being thick, they tend to stay on the surface and are not absorbed: use for thin, delicate items such as fish fillets or chicken breasts. Glazes are similar to pastes, but sweeter. Chutneys and jams, combined with mustards, vinegar and sugar, make lovely tangy glazes. Always brush on a glaze towards the end of cooking, and beware of charring the food, as the sugar quickly caramelizes and burns.

MEXICAN CHILLI PASTE

Enough for 1 medium-large or 2 small chickens.

INGREDIENTS

grated zest and juice of 1 orange, 1 lime and 1 lemon
5 garlic cloves, finely crushed
3 tbsp mild chilli powder
1 tbsp paprika
1 tsp ground cumin
½ tsp dried oregano
¼ tsp ground cinnamon
1 tbsp olive oil
1 tsp salt
½ green chilli, chopped, or more to taste

PREPARATION

Mix ½ teaspoon of each fruit zest and all the juices with the other ingredients, adding more spices if desired. Leave for at least 30 minutes to thicken, before coating the meat.

RUM GLAZE

This glaze is excellent with fattier meats since there is no oil in the mixture. Makes enough to glaze 750g (1½lb) chops or steaks.

INGREDIENTS

100g (3½oz) brown sugar
2 tbsp dark rum
juice of 1 lime or 2 tbsp pineapple juice
grated zest of ½ lime
1 tbsp dry mustard

PREPARATION

1 Mix all the ingredients together.
2 Coat the meat with a dry rub and cook over low heat. Brush on the glaze towards the end of the cooking time.

MANGO-MUSTARD GLAZE

A spicy, sweet-hot glaze is just right for barbecued duck pieces as it keeps the skin crisp. Enough for 1 medium-sized duck, or 750g (1½lb) chops or kebabs.

INGREDIENTS

2½ tbsp mango chutney
1½ tbsp Dijon mustard
1½ tbsp marmalade or apricot jam
several drops of Tabasco or other hot sauce

PREPARATION

1 Mix all the ingredients together, then brush over the cooked food.
2 Return to the barbecue and continue cooking for 15–20 minutes, or until glazed but not burnt.

Mexican Chilli Paste

Mango-mustard Glaze

FLAVOURED BUTTERS

Flavoured butter makes a lovely sauce for simple barbecued food. Serve a slice or two on top of chops, steaks or fish to melt and combine with the hot juices. For a pouring sauce, warm the flavoured butter over the barbecue just before serving. The butters will keep for up to 1 week in the refrigerator, and up to 2 months in the freezer: simply shape into a roll and freeze wrapped in clingfilm.

Coriander & Green Chilli Butter

BASIC SHALLOT BUTTER

INGREDIENTS

125g (4oz) unsalted butter, softened
dash of lemon juice
2 shallots, finely chopped
salt and black pepper

PREPARATION

Combine all the ingredients well, then either serve at room temperature or chill and slice. Place on the hot food and allow it to melt and blend in.

VARIATIONS

TARRAGON BUTTER Add 2 teaspoons of chopped fresh tarragon to the basic shallot butter.
FRESH DILL BUTTER Dill butter is excellent with grilled salmon. Add 2 teaspoons of chopped fresh dill to the basic shallot butter.

Black Olive & Sage Butter

Raspberry & Roasted Garlic Butter

CORIANDER & GREEN CHILLI BUTTER

INGREDIENTS

125g (4oz) unsalted butter, softened
15g (½oz) chopped fresh coriander
3 spring onions, thinly sliced
2 garlic cloves, finely chopped
¼ green chilli, or to taste, finely chopped
dash of lime
pinch of grated lime zest
salt, to taste

PREPARATION

Combine the butter with the coriander, spring onions, garlic, chilli, and lime juice and zest. Mix well and season to taste with salt.

BLACK OLIVE & SAGE BUTTER

INGREDIENTS

125g (4oz) unsalted butter, softened
8–10 fresh sage leaves, chopped
2–3 tbsp black olives in oil, drained and coarsely chopped
2 garlic cloves, finely chopped

PREPARATION

Combine the butter with the other ingredients. Use with veal, or small roast birds.

ROSEMARY-MUSTARD BUTTER

INGREDIENTS

125g (4oz) unsalted butter, softened
1 tbsp French mustard
2 garlic cloves, finely chopped
2 tbsp chopped fresh rosemary
salt and black pepper

PREPARATION

Combine the butter with the other ingredients and season to taste. Use with veal or lamb chops.

Rosemary-mustard Butter

SUN-DRIED TOMATO & BASIL BUTTER

INGREDIENTS

4 garlic cloves, finely chopped
125g (4oz) unsalted butter, softened
5–8 sun-dried tomatoes in oil, diced, plus ½ tsp of the oil
3 tbsp finely chopped fresh basil leaves
salt and black pepper

PREPARATION

Combine the garlic with the butter and sun-dried tomatoes, then work in the basil and season well.

Sun-dried Tomato & Basil Butter

GREEN PEPPERCORN BUTTER

INGREDIENTS

1 tbsp green peppercorns in brine, drained
3 shallots, finely chopped
125g (4oz) unsalted butter, softened
1 tbsp brandy
salt and black pepper

PREPARATION

Pound the peppercorns using a pestle and mortar or with a fork. Add the shallots, butter and brandy and mix well. Season to taste.

Green Peppercorn Butter

RASPBERRY & ROASTED GARLIC BUTTER

INGREDIENTS

6 roasted garlic cloves, peeled and puréed (see page 152)
125g (4oz) unsalted butter, softened
25 fresh raspberries, mashed
dash of raspberry vinegar
salt and black pepper

PREPARATION

Combine the garlic with the butter. Mix well, then work in the raspberries and vinegar, and season.

HAZELNUT BUTTER

INGREDIENTS

125g (4oz) unsalted butter, softened
3 shallots, chopped
4 tbsp chopped hazelnuts, toasted
1–2 tsp pear, cider or raspberry vinegar
salt and black pepper

PREPARATION

Mix the butter with the shallots, hazelnuts and vinegar. Combine with a fork and season well.

OILS & VINEGARS

Keep a selection of oils and vinegars steeped with favourite spices and herbs for marinades and vinaigrettes. Many will keep for up to 1 year in a dark cupboard, though any containing fruits may deteriorate more rapidly. To sterilize containers, boil for 10 minutes, drain, and dry in a low oven.

HERB-INFUSED OIL

This oil will keep for up to 1 month.

INGREDIENTS

a few sprigs of rosemary, thyme and sage
olive oil

PREPARATION

Place the herbs in a sterilized bottle. Gently heat just enough oil to fill the container until bubbles form round the edge. Bottle, then seal when cool.

ANNATTO OIL

This keeps indefinitely, though the colour and aroma fade.

INGREDIENTS

250ml (8fl oz) vegetable oil
4 tbsp annatto seeds

PREPARATION

Gently heat the vegetable oil until bubbles form around the edge. Add the seeds and steep for 2–3 hours. Strain into a sterilized bottle and seal.

OLIVE-OLIVE OIL

This oil will keep for about 2 weeks.

INGREDIENTS

125g (4oz) black olives in oil
several sprigs of fresh rosemary
olive oil, to cover

PREPARATION

Place the olives and rosemary in a sterilized jar and fill with enough olive oil to cover. Seal and leave for several days to develop the flavours.

SPRING ONION-STEEPED OIL

An unusual oil that will keep for up to 1 week in the refrigerator, and up to 2 weeks if strained.

INGREDIENTS

250ml (8fl oz) vegetable oil
8–10 spring onions, thinly sliced

PREPARATION

Gently heat the vegetable oil until tiny bubbles form around the edge. Place the spring onions in a bowl and pour over the heated oil. Cool to room temperature and serve with chicken, fish or oriental dishes.

CLASSIC VINAIGRETTE

This basic recipe can be varied to taste by using any other flavoured vinegar. You can also add 2–3 tablespoons of chopped fresh herbs or a finely chopped shallot.

INGREDIENTS

1 tbsp red or white wine vinegar
1 tsp Dijon mustard
1 garlic clove, finely chopped
3 tbsp extra-virgin olive oil
salt and black pepper

PREPARATION

Whisk together the vinegar, mustard, garlic and oil until well blended and the oil has emulsified, then season to taste.

PEAR VINEGAR

INGREDIENTS

1 ripe pear, chopped or thinly sliced
1 tsp sugar
cider vinegar, to cover
4 tbsp apple or pear juice, optional

PREPARATION

Place the pear and sugar in a large jar. Fill with cider vinegar to cover and add the apple or pear juice, if using. Leave to steep overnight, then strain, squeezing the solids through cheesecloth. Pour into a sterilized bottle and seal.

VERY BERRY VINEGAR

INGREDIENTS

3–4 tbsp blackberries or raspberries
1 tsp sugar
125ml (4fl oz) raspberry or red wine vinegar

PREPARATION

Crush the berries in a bowl and combine with the sugar. Pour over the vinegar and leave overnight. Strain well, pour into a sterilized bottle and seal.

HOT PEPPER VINEGAR

INGREDIENTS

2–3 tbsp crushed dried chillies
70cl bottle of sherry or cider vinegar

PREPARATION

Add the chillies to the vinegar and reseal. It becomes hotter and more flavourful with time.

MIXED HERB VINEGAR

This recipe is a good way of using up small quantities of wine left over after a dinner party. The wine enriches the vinegar, giving it a smoother, deeper flavour. The vinegar will keep for 1 month. To keep it longer, strain off the herbs after they have infused the vinegar for a week.

INGREDIENTS

several sprigs of dried or fresh tarragon, rosemary, thyme, basil or bay leaves
pinch of salt
red or white wine vinegar
red or white wine

PREPARATION

Place the mixed herbs in a sterilized bottle and add the salt. Almost fill the bottle with vinegar, about seven-eighths full, then top up with a little wine, using red wine with red wine vinegar, and white wine with white wine vinegar.

Herb-infused Oil

Mixed Herb Vinegar

Spring Onion-steeped Oil

RECIPES

Every country and culture has specialities that are cooked over an open fire. The following recipes are gathered from far-flung cuisines to reflect the diversity and worldwide appeal of barbecue cookery. Though the seasonings vary from delicate to fiery and the techniques from simple to more complex, the recipes are all enhanced by the aroma of smoke and the distinctive flavours that this method of cooking imparts.

All recipes serve 4 unless otherwise stated.

VEGETABLES

Vegetables taste wonderful cooked on the barbecue, and need only a short time to marinate. Choose from the best in season and vary the flavourings to taste: lemon juice, balsamic vinegar, wine, mustard, a few herbs. Cook enough garlic, peppers and aubergines to last the week and refrigerate – they make wonderful salads and soups.

AUBERGINE & SWEETCORN SOUP

This is a bright-tasting hearty soup that is easy to prepare using barbecued vegetables. It is a particularly good soup to make the day after a barbecue, when the vegetables are already cooked.

INGREDIENTS

½ aubergine, cut lengthways, then scored along the cut side
2 corn-on-the-cobs
2 tbsp olive oil, plus extra for brushing
salt, to taste
1 onion, chopped
3 garlic cloves, finely chopped
750ml (1¼ pints) vegetable or chicken stock
250g (8oz) ripe or canned tomatoes, diced
¼ tsp ground cumin, or to taste
cayenne pepper, to taste

PREPARATION

1 Light the barbecue or preheat a gas barbecue.
2 Brush the aubergine and corn with olive oil, sprinkle with salt, then cook, preferably covered, over medium-low coals until tender, about 10–20 minutes.
3 Remove the vegetables from the barbecue and leave to cool.
4 When cool, dice the aubergine and scrape the corn from the cobs.
5 Heat the olive oil in a pan and sauté the onion and garlic until softened, then add the stock, tomatoes and cumin. Bring to the boil.
6 Reduce the heat and add the aubergine and corn. Continue cooking for another 5–10 minutes to allow the flavours to blend, then season with salt and cayenne to taste. Serve hot.

VARIATION

MEDITERRANEAN FLAVOUR Omit the cumin and cayenne. Add 1 courgette and 1 fennel bulb, grilled and diced, and garnish with shredded basil.

WARM MUSHROOM SALAD WITH PINE NUTS & TARRAGON

This simple-to-prepare dish is full of exciting flavours. Serve it on a bed of crisp greens dressed with nut oil vinaigrette.

INGREDIENTS

6 medium-large mushrooms, about 250–300g (8–10oz)
150g (5oz) mixed curly endive and radicchio, finely sliced
30g (1oz) rocket
2 shallots, chopped
1 tbsp hazelnut or walnut oil
3 tbsp pine nuts
Tarragon Marinade
3 garlic cloves, finely chopped
4 tbsp olive oil
4 tbsp balsamic vinegar
15g (½oz) fresh tarragon, coarsely chopped
salt and black pepper

PREPARATION

1 Light the barbecue or preheat a gas barbecue.
2 To make the marinade, mix together the garlic, olive oil, half the vinegar and half the tarragon. Place the mushrooms in a shallow dish, pour over the marinade and season. Leave for 30 minutes.
3 Drain the mushrooms and cook caps down over a medium heat for 4–5 minutes. Turn and cook the other side for the same time.
4 Meanwhile, combine the sliced endive and radicchio with the rocket and shallots. Toss with the remaining balsamic vinegar and the hazelnut or walnut oil.
5 Serve the hot mushrooms with the crisp greens, and sprinkle with the pine nuts and the remaining tarragon.

CHARGRILLED RADICCHIO WITH GORGONZOLA

Radicchio, endive and lettuce are traditionally cooked on the barbecue in the Venezia region of Italy – the bitter flavour mellows as they cook over the fire. Sprinkled with pungent cheese and herbs, they make a wonderful first course.

INGREDIENTS

125ml (4fl oz) olive oil
5–8 shallots, chopped
4 tbsp white wine vinegar
½ tsp herbes de Provence, crumbled
4 heads radicchio, endive and young cabbage, halved or quartered
salt and black pepper
125g (4oz) Gorgonzola or other blue cheese, sliced
fresh basil leaves, to garnish, optional

PREPARATION

1 Light the barbecue or preheat a gas barbecue.
2 Mix together the olive oil, shallots, vinegar and herbs to make a vinaigrette. Brush the radicchio, endive and cabbage lightly with a little vinaigrette, then cook over a medium-high heat until slightly charred, but not overcooked. They will become slightly limp as they cook.
3 Remove the vegetables from the barbecue and season. Sprinkle with the remaining vinaigrette and serve with the sliced Gorgonzola and the basil leaves, if using.

VARIATION

NORTH ITALIAN BARBECUE Serve grilled radicchio with Rosemary Polenta (see page 134) and herby sausages (see page 111) for an authentic taste. Substitute a tangy chèvre, such as Montrachet, for the Gorgonzola.

GRILLED ASPARAGUS

For those who have never tried barbecuing asparagus, it is a revelation. The slender stalks remain crisp, and their delicate character is surprisingly enhanced by the heat of the flames.

INGREDIENTS

500–750g (1–1½lb) asparagus, ends trimmed
White Wine Marinade
125ml (4fl oz) olive oil
2 tbsp lemon juice or balsamic vinegar
2 tbsp dry white wine
1 tbsp wholegrain or other French mustard
2 garlic cloves, finely chopped
large pinch of fresh thyme or marjoram
salt and black pepper

PREPARATION

1 Light the barbecue or preheat a gas barbecue.
2 Mix together the marinade ingredients in a shallow dish. Add the asparagus and toss well, then leave to marinate for 10–15 minutes.
3 Drain the asparagus and place on the barbecue when medium-hot. Cook until crisp but cooked through, about 3 minutes on each side, depending on the heat of the flames.

SMOKY-SPICY CORN SALAD

Corn, cooked over charcoal then brushed with butter and sprinkled with pepper, is a staple street food of Mexico. Here, it is transformed into a zesty salad.

INGREDIENTS

4 corn-on-the-cobs
15g (½oz) butter, softened
2–3 garlic cloves, finely chopped
2–3 spring onions, thinly sliced
2 tbsp chopped fresh coriander
1 tsp ground cumin
90g (3oz) Salsa (see page 124)
juice of ½ lime
75ml (2½fl oz) olive oil
salt and black pepper

PREPARATION

1 Light the barbecue or preheat a gas barbecue.
2 Spread the corn thinly with butter, then cook covered over medium-hot coals until grill marks form and the corn is tender, about 5–8 minutes.
3 Remove from the heat. When cool enough to handle, scrape the corn off the cobs, combine with the remaining ingredients and season to taste.

BEETROOT WITH MOROCCAN DRESSING

Beetroot cooked over the barbecue grow smoky and rich. You can also use cooked, peeled beetroot.

INGREDIENTS

4–6 raw, unpeeled beetroot or peeled, cooked beetroot
olive oil, for brushing
Moroccan Dressing
3 garlic cloves, finely chopped
1 onion, chopped
1 ripe or canned tomato, chopped
2 tbsp chopped fresh coriander
¼ tsp ground cumin
¼ tsp curry powder
1 tbsp vinegar or lemon juice
3 tbsp olive oil
pinch of sugar
salt and cayenne pepper, to taste

PREPARATION

1 Light the barbecue or preheat a gas barbecue.
2 Brush the beetroot with olive oil and place over medium-low coals. Cook raw beetroot slowly over a low heat until they are easily pierced, 1–1½ hours; ready-cooked beetroot should be placed over the heat just long enough to develop a smoky aroma, about 5 minutes.
3 Remove from the barbecue and peel if necessary, then slice thickly. Blend the dressing ingredients and toss with the beetroot. Taste for seasoning. Serve warm or at room temperature.

VARIATION

GRILLED POTATOES & PUMPKIN Parboil 4–5 large potatoes, then slice thickly. Peel and slice 1 small pumpkin. Marinate in 2 tablespoons of olive oil, 1 tablespoon of lemon juice and 1 chopped garlic clove. Grill until browned, then toss with the Moroccan Dressing.

GRILLED AUBERGINE SLICES

Barbecued aubergines are highly versatile. Cook them whole or sliced, as here, or purée the smoky flesh to use in dips, sauces or soups.

INGREDIENTS

1 aubergine, cut crossways into 1cm (½in) slices
olive oil, for brushing
2 tbsp red or white wine vinegar, or to taste
½ onion, finely chopped
3–4 tbsp chopped fresh parsley
salt and black pepper
2 garlic cloves, finely chopped, optional

PREPARATION

1 Light the barbecue or preheat a gas barbecue.
2 Brush the aubergine slices with olive oil on both sides. Cook over medium-hot coals until the first side has browned and formed grill marks, then turn and cook the other side.
3 Remove from the heat and sprinkle with the vinegar, onion, parsley, salt and pepper, and garlic, if using. Serve at room temperature, either as an appetizer or to accompany roasted meats.

AUBERGINE SALATA

This delectable Middle Eastern dip reminds me of a café I frequented in Tel Aviv as a teenager.

INGREDIENTS

1 medium-large aubergine, halved lengthways
olive oil, for brushing
1 garlic clove, finely chopped
3 tbsp tahini
3 tbsp Greek natural yogurt
juice of ½ lemon
½ tsp cumin seeds
salt, to taste
Tabasco, to taste
lettuce leaves and sprigs of fresh coriander, to garnish

PREPARATION

1 Light the barbecue or preheat a gas barbecue.
2 Score the aubergine deeply without cutting it right through, then brush with olive oil. Cook over medium-hot coals for 10–15 minutes on each side, or until the outside is lightly charred in spots and the flesh is tender. Leave to cool, then dice.
3 Blend together the garlic, tahini, yogurt, lemon juice, cumin seeds, salt and Tabasco, and mix with the aubergine. Serve on a bed of lettuce leaves, garnished with coriander.

CHARGRILLED SPRING ONIONS

INGREDIENTS

16 spring onions, trimmed
Tangy Marinade
2 tbsp French mustard
2 garlic cloves, finely chopped
salt and black pepper
4 tbsp olive oil
juice of ½ lemon

PREPARATION

1 Light the barbecue or preheat a gas barbecue.
2 Combine the marinade ingredients in a shallow dish. Add the spring onions and leave to marinate for about 30 minutes.
3 Drain the spring onions and cook over hot coals until charred on each side and just tender inside.
4 To serve, cut diagonally into bite-sized lengths.

LEEKS WITH CREAMY BEETROOT VINAIGRETTE

This dish is as beautiful as it is delicious. The vinaigrette can be refrigerated for up to 2 days. The leeks could also be served with Mojo Rojo (see page 125).

INGREDIENTS

8 leeks, trimmed
olive oil, for brushing
salt and black pepper
Beetroot Vinaigrette
70ml (2½fl oz) light olive oil
150g (5oz) pickled beetroot, drained and finely chopped
2 shallots, chopped
2 tbsp red or white wine vinegar
pinch of sugar or splash of balsamic vinegar
100ml (3½fl oz) double cream or crème fraîche
3 tbsp chopped chives

PREPARATION

1 Light the barbecue or preheat a gas barbecue.
2 Blanch the leeks in boiling water for about 2 minutes then drain, rinse in cold water and drain well again. Brush with a little olive oil and sprinkle with salt and pepper.
3 To make the vinaigrette, process the olive oil, beetroot, shallots, vinegar and sugar until smooth. Add the cream and process again. Season to taste.
4 Cook the leeks over a hot fire for 2–3 minutes on each side, just long enough to give char marks and an appealing fire-scented aroma.
5 Serve sprinkled generously with chopped chives, with vinaigrette spooned on each plate.

FIRE-COOKED SHALLOTS

Shallots cooked on the barbecue are lovely, their outer layers slightly charred, their insides tender and sweet, and they go well with almost any other dish: steaks, chicken, fish or an assortment of vegetables. They also give a smoky, tropical taste to spicy vegetable soups. Toss an extra handful of shallots on the fire when barbecuing and reserve for the next day's stockpot.

INGREDIENTS

12–16 large shallots, peeled
3 tbsp olive oil
salt and black pepper

PREPARATION

1 Light the barbecue or preheat a gas barbecue. Get 4 skewers ready – wooden skewers should be soaked in cold water for 30 minutes.
2 Blanch the shallots in boiling water for 2–3 minutes then drain, rinse well in cold water and drain again.
3 Thread the shallots on skewers, allowing 3 or 4 per skewer, and brush with olive oil. Cook the shallots on a medium-cool part of the fire for 10–15 minutes, allowing them to char slightly on the outside. Covering enhances the smoky flavour and hastens the cooking time.
4 Remove the shallots from the skewers, sprinkle with salt and pepper and serve immediately.

Fire-roasted
Cherry
Tomatoes

Fire-cooked
Shallots

FIRE-ROASTED CHERRY TOMATOES

Skewer the tomatoes to keep them from falling into the fire and for easy removal from the grill.

INGREDIENTS

24–30 cherry tomatoes
salt
2 tbsp olive oil
2–3 garlic cloves, finely chopped

PREPARATION

1 Light the barbecue or preheat a gas barbecue. Get 6 skewers ready – wooden skewers should be soaked in cold water for 30 minutes.
2 Thread the tomatoes on the skewers, allowing 4 or 5 tomatoes per skewer.
3 Cook over medium-hot coals, covered if possible, for about 5–8 minutes, or until the tomatoes have heated through and split their skins slightly.
4 Serve immediately, sprinkled with salt, olive oil and garlic, or with a dab of flavoured butter (see pages 42–43).

GREEN BEANS WITH GARLIC BUTTER

Green beans are fantastic cooked on the barbecue. Skewer them, or place on a fine wire mesh, to prevent them falling into the fire.

INGREDIENTS

500g (1lb) green beans
60g (2oz) butter
4 garlic cloves, chopped or crushed
salt and black pepper

PREPARATION

1 Light the barbecue or preheat a gas barbecue. Get 6–8 skewers ready – wooden skewers should be soaked in cold water for 30 minutes.
2 Blanch the beans very quickly in boiling water, just until they turn bright green. Drain, rinse well in cold water and drain again.
3 Skewer the beans crossways, threading about 5–8 beans on each skewer.
4 Warm the butter in a small pan until melted, then remove from the heat and add the garlic. Brush a small amount of garlic butter on the green beans and keep the remainder warm.
5 Cook the beans quickly over medium-hot coals, about 2–3 minutes on each side. Remove the skewers and serve with the remaining garlic butter poured over.

FAR EASTERN BROCCOLI

Broccoli, blanched then quickly barbecued, is a delicious surprise. Cook covered to encourage a smoky flavour.

INGREDIENTS

1kg (2lb) broccoli, divided into florets,
stems peeled
Oriental Marinade
1 tbsp sugar
1–2 tsp grated ginger root
1 garlic clove, finely chopped
3 tbsp dark soy sauce
2 tbsp sesame oil
1 tbsp balsamic vinegar

PREPARATION

1 Blanch the broccoli quickly in boiling water, just until it turns bright green. Drain immediately and rinse well in cold water or plunge into iced water. Drain well again and place in a shallow dish.
2 Mix the marinade ingredients, pour over the broccoli and leave to marinate for up to 3 hours.
3 Light the barbecue or preheat a gas barbecue.
4 Drain the broccoli and reserve the marinade. Cook the broccoli over hot coals for about 1 minute on each side.
5 Arrange the broccoli on serving plates and pour over the reserved marinade.

ROASTED CARROTS

Cooking carrots over the fire concentrates their sweet flavour and a ginger butter amplifies it.

INGREDIENTS

4 large thick carrots or 8 smaller carrots
salt
45g (1½oz) butter
1 garlic clove, finely chopped
1 piece preserved ginger, chopped, plus 1 tbsp
syrup from the jar

PREPARATION

1 Light the barbecue or preheat a gas barbecue.
2 Blanch the carrots in boiling salted water until tender but still crunchy, about 6 minutes. Drain and rinse in cold water. Cut thick carrots in half lengthways.
3 Heat the butter and garlic for 3 minutes, then add the preserved ginger and the syrup. Remove from the heat and toss the carrots in the mixture.
4 Cook over medium-hot coals, turning once or twice until lightly browned, about 6–8 minutes.

STUFFED PEPPERS

*Chillies and peppers roasted on the barbecue develop
a deliciously smoky flavour. The skin separates
from the flesh, especially if cooked under a cover,
making them easy to peel. (This can be done
ahead of time.) Serve with a salad of mixed leaves,
sprinkled with spring onions and coriander,
as a spicy starter, or with Butterflied Leg of Lamb
(see page 96) as a light lunch.*

INGREDIENTS

8–10 mild chilli peppers, such as Anaheim, Poblano,
Thai, Serrano or European chillies, or 4 green peppers
4 tbsp olive oil
2 tbsp red or white wine vinegar
3 garlic cloves, finely chopped
1 tbsp fresh oregano, chopped, or
½ tsp dried oregano or marjoram
salt and black pepper
several generous pinches of cayenne pepper
125g (4oz) mild goat's cheese, or more as needed

PREPARATION

1 Light the barbecue or preheat a gas barbecue.
2 Roast the peppers over medium-hot coals,
turning every few minutes until the outside is
evenly charred but the flesh is not burnt through,
about 8–10 minutes. Covering the barbecue will
encourage the skin to separate from the flesh.
3 Place the peppers in a bowl or plastic bag and
seal so that the heat steams off the charred skins.
Leave for 30–45 minutes to cool. This is best done
ahead of time for maximum flavour and aroma.
4 When cool, peel the peppers, make a lengthways
slit in the side, and remove and discard the core
and seeds. Arrange in a shallow dish.
5 Blend half the oil and vinegar with the
garlic, oregano or marjoram, salt and pepper, and
cayenne. Pour over the peppers. Leave for 2 hours
at room temperature, or overnight in the
refrigerator.
6 Drain the peppers, reserving the marinade, and
stuff each one with a tablespoon of goat's cheese. If
cooking green peppers, stuff each with a quarter
of the cheese, using more to fill them if necessary.
7 Arrange the peppers in a baking dish and pour
over the marinade. Place over medium coals,
covered, or under the grill for 4–5 minutes, just
long enough to melt the cheese.
8 If making a salad, toss the salad leaves with the
remaining oil and vinegar.
9 Serve the stuffed peppers with a salad of mixed
leaves, sprinkled with sliced spring onions and
chopped coriander.

Garlic

*Red wine
vinegar*

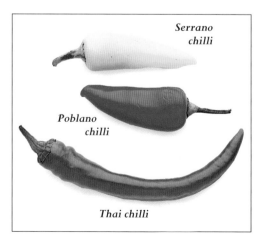

Olive oil

*Serrano
chilli*

*Poblano
chilli*

Thai chilli

Oregano

Salt

Black
pepper

Cayenne
pepper

Goat's cheese

ARTICHOKES WITH TOMATO-TAPENADE VINAIGRETTE

This is my own interpretation of a Sicilian peasant dish: the smoke emphasizes the distinctive character of the artichoke. The Tomato-tapenade Vinaigrette is especially good with artichokes, but mayonnaise, Aïoli (see page 66), or a flavoured butter (see pages 42–43) could also be served.

INGREDIENTS

4 artichokes, stems peeled and trimmed and
sharp leaf points removed
10 garlic cloves, finely chopped
50g (1½oz) fresh parsley, chopped
175ml (6fl oz) olive oil
3 tbsp vinegar
salt and black pepper
Tomato-tapenade Vinaigrette
1–2 garlic cloves, finely chopped
2 tsp tapenade or other black olive paste
1 tbsp red wine vinegar
1 tbsp tomato purée
1 tbsp chopped fresh parsley
75ml (2½fl oz) olive oil

PREPARATION

1 Light the barbecue or preheat a gas barbecue.
2 Cook the artichokes in boiling water for 15 minutes, then drain upside-down. Open up the artichoke leaves and pull out the pale inner leaves. Using a teaspoon, scrape out the fuzzy choke (see page 152) and discard. Place in a dish.
3 Mix together the garlic, parsley, oil, vinegar, salt and pepper. Spoon the mixture into each artichoke, placing some between the leaves. Pour any remaining mixture over the artichokes and leave for a few minutes to marinate.
4 Cook the artichokes over medium-hot coals, turning every so often until they are cooked through and lightly charred in places (the outer leaves will be discarded as you eat the artichokes).
5 To make the vinaigrette, blend the garlic with the tapenade, vinegar, tomato purée and parsley. Whisk in the oil (it will need to be restirred just before serving).
6 Serve the artichokes with the vinaigrette as a dipping sauce for the leaves.

VARIATION

MEDITERRANEAN ARTICHOKES & SWORDFISH
Instead of the vinaigrette, use the Mediterranean Marinade (see page 59) and add 4 swordfish steaks. Marinate for 3 hours at room temperature then grill over hot coals for about 10 minutes, turning once.

STUFFED AUBERGINE

This dish hails from Sardinia, where aubergines are stuffed with all kinds of savoury ingredients, including cheese, salami, ham and herbs. I have simplified the stuffing to Pesto (see page 124) and cheese. It serves 4 as an appetizer, with roasted peppers, olives and crusty bread, or 2 as a main course.

INGREDIENTS

3 garlic cloves, finely chopped
175g (6oz) full-flavour cheese, such as Fontina
or mature Cheddar, grated
3–4 tbsp Pesto (see page 124)
1 medium-large aubergine

PREPARATION

1 Light the barbecue or preheat a gas barbecue.
2 Mix together the garlic, cheese and Pesto.
3 Cut 4 or 5 slashes in the aubergine to form deep pockets. Open up each slash a little with your fingers, then fill with several tablespoons of the cheese mixture.
4 Place the stuffed aubergine in a heatproof baking dish, then spread the remaining cheese mixture over the top. Cook over medium coals, preferably covered, for about 35 minutes or until the aubergine is cooked through, the cheese has melted and the cheese topping is crusty.

VARIATION

Leftovers make lovely sandwiches on crusty bread, accompanied by sliced tomatoes, salami and olives.

New Potatoes & Yams with Mojo Sauces

Mojo sauces are zesty garlicky sauces from the Canary Islands, traditionally eaten with all types of grilled meats, poultry and fish, as well as with the classic dish of papas arrugadas, or "wrinkled potatoes", so called because cooking the potatoes in salty water makes the skins wrinkle up. Here the sauces are paired with a selection of vegetables for a robust starter; add 1–2 lamb chops per person for a full meal.

INGREDIENTS

500g (1lb) new potatoes
2 yams, sliced crossways and halved
olive oil for brushing
salt for sprinkling
1 yellow pepper, cored, deseeded and cut into strips
To serve
Mojo Rojo and Mojo Verde (see page 125)

PREPARATION

1 Light the barbecue or preheat a gas barbecue.
2 Parboil the potatoes and yams until they just begin to give when pierced with a skewer or fork. Drain and leave to cool for at least 30 minutes.
3 Brush the potatoes and yams with olive oil and sprinkle with salt. Cook over medium-hot coals, turning occasionally, until the vegetables develop grill marks from the barbecue and are cooked through, about 20 minutes.
4 Arrange the vegetables on a platter with one or both of the Mojo sauces and garnish with the strips of yellow pepper.

VARIATION

STEAK WITH CORN & MOJO VERDE Brush 4 steaks and 4 corn cobs with Mojo sauce then with olive oil. Grill over hot coals until the corn is tender and the steaks are browned, but still rare inside, about 4–5 minutes. Serve with Mojo sauce on the side.

MAPLE-ROASTED SWEET POTATOES

The flesh of sweet potatoes varies from almost white to a deep yellowy orange. Choose plump ones with smooth unwrinkled skins and a strong orange colour: the brighter coloured ones have more flavour.

INGREDIENTS

4 sweet potatoes, halved lengthways
90g (3oz) butter, softened
90ml (3fl oz) maple syrup

PREPARATION

1 Light the barbecue or preheat a gas barbecue.
2 Steam or boil the sweet potatoes until semi-tender, about 8–10 minutes, depending on size. Drain and leave to cool to room temperature.
3 Blend together the butter and maple syrup.
4 Score the cut sides of the potatoes, then spread some of the butter mixture over all sides.
5 Cook over medium coals, turning once or twice, allowing the outsides to brown and develop grill marks, about 6–8 minutes on each side.
6 Remove from the barbecue and serve, spread with the remaining butter and maple syrup.

FIRE-BAKED POTATOES

When I lived on a Greek island, the local café served fire-roasted potatoes as part of their meze. *The patron fished a few from the fire, cut them into chunks, sprinkled them with salt and served them up with a plate of olives and another of greens doused in vinegar. For a richer dish, serve with sour cream seasoned with chopped spring onions, chives and shallots.*

INGREDIENTS

4 medium-large baking potatoes, washed but unpeeled
vegetable oil, for brushing

PREPARATION

1 Light the barbecue or preheat a gas barbecue.
2 Prick the potatoes once or twice so they won't burst during cooking, then brush with a little oil.
3 Place the potatoes over medium-low coals and leave, preferably covered, for 40–60 minutes, turning occasionally to make sure that they cook evenly. Alternatively, place in a mound of slow coals and leave for 1–2 hours, or until meltingly tender inside. Test with a skewer after 1 hour.
4 Serve hot with either a salad of greens, or sour cream flavoured with chopped spring onions, chives and shallots.

TWO-BEAN CHEESEBURGERS WITH CHILLI AIOLI

These are good the way they are, or serve them sandwiched in a wholegrain bun or crusty ciabatta roll.

INGREDIENTS

400g (13oz) can black beans or chick-peas, drained
400g (13oz) can borlotti or kidney beans, drained
3 garlic cloves, finely chopped
1 onion, grated
1 egg, lightly beaten
75–100g (2½–3oz) dry breadcrumbs
¾ tsp ground cumin
4 tbsp chopped fresh coriander
salt and cayenne pepper, to taste
vegetable oil, for brushing
175g (6oz) mature Cheddar, thinly sliced
To serve
Red Chilli Aïoli (see page 124)
lettuce
pickled chillies

PREPARATION

1 Light the barbecue or preheat a gas barbecue.
2 Purée the beans in a food processor until they form a chunky paste. Mix in the garlic, onion, egg, breadcrumbs, cumin and coriander then season with salt and cayenne pepper.
3 Form the mixture into 6–10 patties. Brush with oil and cook over medium-hot coals until lightly browned, about 4–5 minutes on each side. When the second side is half browned, about 2 minutes, top each patty with a slice of cheese and continue to cook until the cheese melts.
4 Serve spread with the Aïoli, accompanied by lettuce and pickled chillies.

TOFU TIKKA IN TOMATO-PEA MASALA

Cooking on the barbecue firms up tofu, making it perfect for cutting into smaller pieces and then simmering in a sauce. Here, tikka spices permeate the bland tofu along with the smoke of the fire. The masala sauce tastes terrific with the smoky spiced tofu.

INGREDIENTS

285g (9½oz) tofu cake
Tikka Marinade (see page 35)
Tomato-pea Masala Sauce
30g (1oz) butter
1 onion, chopped
3 garlic cloves, chopped
1 tsp chopped ginger root
¼ tsp fennel seeds
¼ tsp garam masala or curry powder
¼ tsp ground coriander
¼ tsp ground cumin
pinch of crushed dried chillies
250g (8oz) chopped canned tomatoes
125g (4oz) fresh peas, shelled and blanched
or frozen peas
150g (5oz) fromage frais
salt
cayenne pepper, to taste

PREPARATION

1 Cut the tofu into 4 or 6 large chunks, place in a shallow dish and rub with the marinade. Leave to marinate for 1 hour at room temperature, or overnight in the refrigerator.
2 Light the barbecue or preheat a gas barbecue.
3 Cook the tofu over medium coals, preferably covered, for about 4–5 minutes on each side.
4 Remove the tofu from the barbecue then leave to cool. When cool, cut into bite-sized pieces. Barbecued tofu is best the next day when the flavours have had time to soak in.
5 To make the sauce, melt half the butter in a large frying pan and sauté the onion until soft, about 5 minutes. Add the garlic, ginger and fennel seeds and cook for another minute or two.
6 Stir in the garam masala, coriander, cumin, crushed chillies and the remaining butter. Cook for a few minutes, then add the tomatoes and peas. Bring to the boil, then reduce the heat and add the tofu pieces.
7 Heat through the tofu mixture, then gently stir in the fromage frais, taking care not to break up the tofu. Season with salt and cayenne and serve immediately.

MEDITERRANEAN KEBABS

Any Mediterranean vegetable could be added to these colourful and tasty kebabs.

INGREDIENTS

3–4 courgettes, cut crossways into
1cm (½in) slices
1 large yellow pepper, cored, deseeded and
cut into bite-sized pieces
16 cherry tomatoes
2 onions, cut into chunks
several sprigs of thyme or marjoram
Mediterranean Marinade
5 garlic cloves, finely chopped
3 tbsp balsamic vinegar
90ml (3fl oz) olive oil
2 tbsp chopped fresh marjoram or thyme
salt and black pepper

PREPARATION

1 Light the barbecue or preheat a gas barbecue. Get 8 skewers ready – wooden skewers should be soaked in cold water for 30 minutes.
2 Thread the vegetables on to the skewers with the herb sprigs, alternating the colours, and place in a shallow dish. Combine the marinade ingredients and pour over the skewers. Leave to marinate for 30 minutes.
3 Drain the kebabs, reserving the marinade, and cook over hot coals for about 5 minutes on each side. Serve hot, with the marinade poured over.

FISH

There are few ways of preparing fish and seafood as appealing or versatile as cooking over hot coals. The method is simple and convenient, needing only an easily prepared marinade, and a suitable relish or sauce to serve with the dish – and because you are cooking outside, no fishy smells linger in the kitchen afterwards. For best results, oil the grill well, and use a wire basket for fragile fillets or whole fish, so that they can be turned easily without disintegrating.

FISH KEBABS

Use fish of differing colours and textures for these kebabs. Shellfish such as prawns can also be added. The typically Italian inclusion of breadcrumbs helps coat the fish and protects it against the hot fire.

INGREDIENTS

175g (6oz) tuna steak, cut into bite-sized pieces
175g (6oz) salmon steaks, skinned, boned and cut into bite-sized pieces
175g (6oz) cod or other white fish, skinned, boned and cut into bite-sized pieces
5 garlic cloves, finely chopped
1½ tbsp capers, crushed
juice of ½ lemon
4 tbsp olive oil
2 tbsp chopped fresh basil, plus several sprigs to garnish
4 tbsp dry breadcrumbs
salt and black pepper

PREPARATION

1 Place the tuna, salmon and cod on a large plate or in a shallow dish.
2 Sprinkle the fish with the garlic, capers, lemon juice, olive oil, chopped basil, the breadcrumbs, salt and pepper. Turn the fish to coat well with the flavourings, then leave for at least an hour to marinate at room temperature, or for up to 12 hours in the refrigerator.
3 Light the barbecue or preheat a gas barbecue. Get 8 skewers ready – wooden skewers should be soaked in cold water for 30 minutes.
4 Thread the fish on to the skewers, alternating the different types of fish. Cook over hot coals, preferably covered, until the kebabs are cooked through, about 2–3 minutes on each side.
5 Serve the kebabs immediately, garnished with basil sprigs.

MUSTARD-FLAVOURED MACKEREL

Mackerel, being strongly flavoured and oily in texture, is excellent for barbecuing. Care should be taken, however, as mackerel can fall apart on the grill: oil the surface well before placing the fish on it; alternatively, place the fish on a piece of foil or in a wire basket over the grill.

INGREDIENTS

2 whole mackerel, cleaned and boned, or 4 mackerel fillets
2 garlic cloves, finely chopped
3–4 tbsp wholegrain mustard
2–3 tbsp olive oil
1–2 tsp sherry vinegar
salt and black pepper
2 tsp chopped chives or fresh parsley

PREPARATION

1 Lay the mackerel flat on a plate.
2 Combine the garlic, mustard, olive oil and vinegar, then spread over both sides of the fish. Leave to marinate for 30 minutes.
3 Light the barbecue or preheat a gas barbecue.
4 Sprinkle the fish with salt and pepper, then cook over hot coals for about 4–6 minutes on each side, or until it browns lightly and sizzles.
5 Lift carefully off the barbecue and serve immediately, sprinkled with the chives or parsley.

VARIATION

JAPANESE GRILLED MACKEREL Lay the mackerel fillets in a shallow baking dish. Combine 3 tablespoons each of mirin or medium dry sherry and dark soy sauce with 2 chopped garlic cloves. Bring to the boil, then spoon the hot marinade over the fish and leave for 30 minutes. Grill the fish over hot coals for 4–6 minutes on each side, until lightly brown and sizzling.

TROUT WRAPPED IN VINE LEAVES WITH BEAN SAUCE

The haunting aroma of vine leaves permeates the flesh of the trout, giving it a distinctive flavour. Be sure to peel the broad beans; peeling reveals their lovely green colour and removes the tough outer skin.

INGREDIENTS

5 garlic cloves, finely chopped
125ml (4fl oz) olive oil
juice of 1½ lemons
4 trout, about 300g (10oz) each, gutted
salt and black pepper
20–24 vine leaves, enough to make 4 parcels; if using leaves preserved in brine, rinse well, then pat dry with kitchen paper
large pinch of sage, fresh chopped, or dried
60g (2oz) butter
fresh herb sprigs, to scent the barbecue
90g (3oz) baby broad beans, blanched and peeled
lemon slices and fresh sage sprigs, to garnish

PREPARATION

1 Mix together half the garlic, 2 tablespoons of oil and the juice of the half lemon and use to rub the trout inside and out. Season to taste. Stuff each trout with a few rolled-up vine leaves and a little sage, then wrap in vine leaves, leaving the head and tail free (see page 154). If necessary, use string to hold the leaves in place. Leave for 1–2 hours.

2 To make the sauce, warm the remaining oil, then add the remaining garlic. When fragrant but not brown, remove from the heat and add the butter.

3 Light the barbecue or preheat a gas barbecue.

4 Cook the trout over medium-hot coals, adding the herb sprigs to the fire. Turn gently after about 10 minutes. When the leaves are charred around the edges and the fish is firm to the touch, another 5–10 minutes, remove from the heat.

5 Add the beans to the sauce with the juice of 1 lemon. Season and gently warm through.

6 Remove any heavily charred leaves and serve the trout with the bean sauce. Garnish with lemon slices and sage sprigs.

COD WITH SUN-DRIED TOMATO RELISH

*Cod is delicious served with this savoury paste.
When I sampled this dish in the middle of
winter – in fact, in the midst of a snowstorm – my
first thought was that it tasted of summer.*

INGREDIENTS

*4 cod fillets, about 750g (1½lb)
salt and black pepper
8–12 basil leaves, shredded
30g (1oz) flaked almonds*
Sun-dried Tomato Relish
*2 garlic cloves, finely chopped or crushed
10–15 sun-dried tomatoes
1 tbsp capers
3 tbsp olive oil, plus extra for brushing
1–2 tsp sherry vinegar*

PREPARATION

1 Light the barbecue or preheat a gas barbecue.
2 To make the relish, purée the garlic using a
pestle and mortar or food processor, then add the
sun-dried tomatoes, capers, olive oil and sherry
vinegar. Season with pepper and set aside.
3 Brush the cod with a little olive oil, then
sprinkle with salt and pepper. Place over hot coals,
preferably in a wire basket, and cook for 2–3
minutes on each side. Take care that the fish does
not overcook, or it will fall apart when you lift it
from the barbecue.
4 To serve, spread each fillet lightly with a little
Sun-dried Tomato Relish, then sprinkle with the
basil and almonds. Serve immediately.

VARIATION

COD A LA NIÇOISE Omit the flaked almonds and
instead serve the cod sprinkled with the basil and
surrounded by a handful of young beans, blanched
until tender but still crisp, and mixed salad leaves,
all tossed in a little olive oil and vinegar.

CURRIED COD WITH LIME

*The longer you leave the fish to marinate in the spicy
mixture, the more flavoured it will be. I often
prepare this dish the night before and leave the cod
to marinate for 24 hours in the refrigerator. The
following evening the fish is ready to be barbecued
for a quickly prepared dinner.*

INGREDIENTS

*½ onion or 5 shallots, finely chopped
2 garlic cloves, finely chopped
½ green chilli, such as Jalapeño, Kenya or Serrano,
chopped, or to taste
2 tsp chopped ginger root
1 tsp paprika
1 tsp curry powder or garam masala
½ tsp ground coriander
½ tsp ground cumin
juice of ½ lime
2 tbsp plain yogurt
salt
4 cod fillets, about 750g (1½lb)
Coriander & Green Chilli Butter
(see page 42), cut into thin pats
½ lime, cut into wedges*

PREPARATION

1 Purée the onion, garlic, chilli and ginger until
it is a fragrant paste, then add the paprika, curry
powder, coriander and cumin and mix in the lime
juice. Stir in the yogurt and season with salt.
2 Place the fish fillets in a shallow dish and rub on
both sides with the curry mixture until well
coated. Leave to marinate at room temperature
for up to 3 hours, or overnight in the refrigerator.
3 Light the barbecue or preheat a gas barbecue.
4 Cook the cod over hot coals for 4–6 minutes,
preferably covered and in a fish basket, turning
only once so that fish does not fall apart.
5 Serve hot, with a pat of Coriander & Green
Chilli Butter on each fish fillet and a wedge of lime.

Cajun Spice Fish & Golden Courgettes

Cajun spices give a delightful zest to cod. Skewers of tiny golden and green squash or slices of pumpkin could be used instead of the courgettes. Serve with a spoonful of Creole Remoulade (see right) instead of the flavoured butter, if you prefer.

INGREDIENTS

4 cod fillets, about 750g (1½lb)
Cajun Spice Rub (see page 40)
2 yellow courgettes, sliced into 3mm (⅛in) thick strips
Sun-dried Tomato & Basil Butter (see page 43)
2 spring onions, thinly sliced
1–2 tbsp chopped fresh coriander

PREPARATION

1 Coat the cod fillets on both sides with three-quarters of the Cajun Spice Rub. Place in a shallow dish and leave to marinate at room temperature for at least 1 hour, or overnight in the refrigerator.
2 Light the barbecue or preheat a gas barbecue.
3 Cook the cod fillets over hot coals, preferably in a wire basket, for 2–3 minutes on each side until the fish feels firm, turning once.
4 When the fish is half cooked, dust the courgettes with the remaining Cajun Spice Rub and place on the grill. Cook for 2–3 minutes, turning several times, until lightly charred.
5 Serve immediately, with a slice of Sun-dried Tomato & Basil Butter (see page 43) and a sprinkling of spring onions and chopped coriander.

Haddock with Creole Remoulade

INGREDIENTS

30g (1oz) butter
3–4 tbsp black olive paste
2 garlic cloves, finely chopped
750g (1½lb) haddock fillets or steaks
Creole Remoulade
2 spring onions, thinly sliced
4–6 tbsp mayonnaise
1 garlic clove, finely chopped
2–3 tsp wholegrain mustard
1 tsp capers, lightly crushed
½ tsp paprika
black pepper
1–2 tbsp olive oil
juice of ¼ lemon, or to taste

PREPARATION

1 Melt the butter, then remove from the heat. Mix with the olive paste and the garlic.
2 Coat the fish fillets with the olive mixture, place in a shallow dish and leave for at least 30 minutes.
3 Light the barbecue or preheat a gas barbecue.
4 To make the remoulade, mix together the spring onions, mayonnaise, garlic, mustard, capers, paprika and black pepper. Stir in the olive oil until it is absorbed, then add lemon juice to taste.
5 Cook the fish over hot coals, preferably in a wire basket, for 2–3 minutes on each side, until lightly browned. Serve the fillets immediately with the remoulade.

Skate with Caper & Brown Butter Sauce

Skate is an excellent fish for the barbecue, being firm-fleshed, and its unusual, wing shape is also very appealing. This classic dish takes on an added dimension when cooked in this way.

INGREDIENTS

4 skate wing portions, about 750g (1½lb)
salt and black pepper
15g (½oz) butter
Caper & Brown Butter Sauce
45g (1½oz) butter
1–1½ tbsp flavoured vinegar, such as raspberry, walnut or tarragon
1 tbsp capers
2 tbsp chopped fresh parsley

PREPARATION

1 Light the barbecue or preheat a gas barbecue.
2 Season the fish and dot with the butter. Set aside while you make the sauce.
3 To make the sauce, melt the butter over medium heat until it turns brown and nutty. Do not let it burn.
4 Add the vinegar to the butter then remove from the heat. Set aside and keep warm.
5 Place the skate on a well-oiled grill, or preferably in a wire basket. Cook, covered if possible, over hot coals until the edges are lightly browned and the fish feels firmish to the touch, about 8 minutes. If the fish is cooked covered, there will be no need to turn it.
6 Remove the fish carefully and pour over the sauce. Sprinkle with the capers and parsley and serve immediately.

Herb-cured Barbecued Salmon

A light curing with salt and herbs firms and seasons the salmon. The centre of the steaks should appear slightly underdone, for maximum flavour and most appealing texture. Serve with a salad of pickled cucumber sprinkled with dill, and black bread with butter.

INGREDIENTS

4 salmon steaks, 175–200g (6–7oz) each
4 tbsp coarse salt
1 tbsp sugar
15g (½oz) chopped fresh tarragon
2 tbsp chopped fresh dill or fennel
2 tbsp melted butter
black pepper, to taste
lemon wedges, to garnish

PREPARATION

1 Place the salmon steaks in a shallow dish and add the salt, sugar, half the tarragon and half the dill or fennel. Turn to coat well, then leave to marinate at room temperature for 3–5 hours, or overnight in the refrigerator.
2 Light the barbecue or preheat a gas barbecue.
3 Brush the salt-sugar-herb mixture off the salmon steaks. Rinse the steaks in cool water, then dry with kitchen paper. Brush them with half the melted butter.
4 Cook the steaks over hot coals for 2–3 minutes until just brown, then turn. Cook on the other side until they feel fairly firm but slightly underdone.
5 Serve the steaks immediately, drizzled with the remaining butter and sprinkled with black pepper and the remaining tarragon and dill. Garnish with lemon wedges.

Salmon with Chermoula

Chermoula is a Moroccan seasoning paste used for marinating food, especially fish. I also like using this mixture with whole salmon, tucking it into the cavity to permeate the flesh with its aroma and flavour.

INGREDIENTS

4 salmon steaks, 175–200g (6–7oz) each
Chermoula
4 garlic cloves, finely chopped
½ green chilli, such as Jalapeño, Kenya or Serrano, finely chopped
3–4 tomatoes, chopped
4 tbsp chopped fresh coriander
4 tbsp chopped fresh parsley
3 tbsp olive oil
juice of ½ lemon
½ tsp each ground cumin and curry powder
salt, to taste

PREPARATION

1 To make the Chermoula, combine the garlic, chilli, tomatoes, coriander, parsley, 2 tablespoons of olive oil, the lemon juice, cumin and curry powder. Process until smooth and season to taste.
2 Combine the remaining olive oil with half the Chermoula in a shallow dish. Add the salmon steaks and turn until well coated. Leave to marinate for 1–3 hours at room temperature.
3 Light the barbecue or preheat a gas barbecue.
4 Cook the salmon over hot coals, preferably covered, for 8–10 minutes, turning once, until the salmon is opaque and feels firmish to the touch.
5 Serve immediately, accompanied by the remaining Chermoula.

SALMON & BACON KEBABS WITH TARRAGON SAUCE

Serve as an appetizer while the rest of the dinner cooks on the barbecue, or as a main course, accompanied by a bowl of Garlic & Spring Onion Mash (see page 133) and a crisp green salad.

INGREDIENTS

375g (12oz) salmon steaks, cut into about 30 cubes
8 rashers smoked streaky bacon
8 cherry tomatoes
2 tbsp olive oil
1 tbsp balsamic vinegar
Tarragon Sauce
3–5 shallots, chopped
1 garlic clove, finely chopped
125ml (4fl oz) dry white wine
1 tomato, diced
3 tbsp dried tarragon, or 15g (½oz) chopped fresh
1 tbsp chopped fresh parsley
125ml (4fl oz) fish stock
salt and black pepper

PREPARATION

1 To make the sauce, combine half the shallots with the garlic, wine, tomato, tarragon and parsley in a small pan. Bring to the boil and cook over a high heat for 3–4 minutes until it is reduced to about 2 tablespoons of liquid.
2 Add the stock and continue to cook over a high heat until it reduces again to about 4 tablespoons. Strain and leave to cool. Season with salt and pepper; it should have a strong, slightly sour and herby taste.
3 Light the barbecue or preheat a gas barbecue. Get 8 skewers ready – wooden skewers should be soaked in cold water for 30 minutes.
4 Thread the skewers, using 1 slice of bacon and 3–4 cubes of salmon per skewer. Alternate the bacon and the salmon, letting the bacon wind its way from end to end of each skewer so that it bastes the salmon as it cooks. Place a cherry tomato at the end of each skewer.
5 Lay the skewers on a plate and sprinkle with the remaining shallots, the olive oil and balsamic vinegar, and 3 tablespoons of the Tarragon Sauce. Leave for about 10 minutes or until ready to cook.
6 Place the skewers over hot coals and cook quickly, turning several times, until the bacon is well-browned and the salmon is cooked through, about 6 minutes. Drizzle each skewer with a little of the remaining sauce. Serve immediately with Garlic & Spring Onion Mash (see page 133) and a crisp green salad.

SALMON BURGERS WITH PESTO & GRILLED ASPARAGUS

These are delightfully elegant burgers compared to the standard hamburger. Asparagus, crisp and hot from the barbecue, and a herby Pesto (see page 124) make this a lovely choice for the first warm evenings of spring.

INGREDIENTS

500g (1lb) salmon fillet or steaks, boned
juice of ½ lemon
60–90g (2–3oz) softened butter
60g (2oz) soft breadcrumbs, or more as needed
1 tsp chopped fresh parsley
3 shallots, finely chopped
salt and black pepper
½ bundle asparagus, ends trimmed
1 tbsp olive oil or melted butter
4 tbsp Pesto (see page 124), or to taste

PREPARATION

1 Chop the salmon into small pieces, then mince finely in a food processor or by hand.
2 Place the salmon in a bowl and add half the lemon juice. Using a fork, work the butter, breadcrumbs, parsley, shallots, salt and pepper into the salmon, making sure the mixture is thoroughly combined. Form into 4 patties, wrap them in clingfilm, then chill in the refrigerator for at least an hour to firm them up.
3 Light the barbecue or preheat a gas barbecue.
4 Sprinkle the remaining lemon juice over the asparagus, then drizzle with the olive oil. Sprinkle with salt and pepper. Grill the salmon patties and the asparagus over the hot coals, preferably in a wire basket, for about 2 minutes on each side.
5 Serve the patties with a dollop of Pesto on the side, or spread some over each patty.

MONKFISH KEBABS WITH AIOLI

*The clean, refreshing quality of tangy Aïoli
makes a delicious foil to rich monkfish.*

INGREDIENTS

*750g (1½lb) monkfish steaks, cut into about 30 chunks
salt, to taste
2 tbsp olive oil*

Aïoli

*1 garlic clove, crushed
1 large free-range egg
1 tbsp French mustard
juice of ½ lemon
salt and cayenne pepper, to taste
200-250ml (7–8fl oz) olive oil*

PREPARATION

1 Light the barbecue or preheat a gas barbecue. Get 8 skewers ready – wooden skewers should be soaked in cold water for 30 minutes.

2 To make the Aïoli, blend the garlic in a food processor with the egg, mustard, lemon juice, salt and cayenne.

3 Slowly blend in the oil, a drop or two at a time. Once half the oil has been absorbed, add the rest in a thin stream, allowing it to emulsify before adding more. Blend until thickened, then refrigerate.

4 Thread the monkfish on the skewers. Sprinkle with salt, then brush with olive oil. Cook over hot coals for 3–4 minutes on each side, according to thickness. Serve with the Aïoli, and Mojo Rojo (see page 125) if liked.

SWORDFISH STEAKS FROM THE ISLE OF CAPRI

INGREDIENTS

4 swordfish steaks, about 750g (1½lb)
olive oil, for brushing
Tomato Sauce
400g (13oz) canned chopped tomatoes
3–5 garlic cloves, finely chopped
125ml (4fl oz) olive oil
red wine vinegar, to taste
2 tsp anchovy paste, or to taste
black pepper or cayenne pepper, to taste
handful of chopped fresh herbs, such as basil,
parsley, marjoram, thyme, mint

PREPARATION

1 Light the barbecue or preheat a gas barbecue.
2 To make the sauce, combine the tomatoes, garlic, olive oil, vinegar, anchovy paste and black pepper or cayenne to taste. Stir in the herbs.
3 Brush the steaks with olive oil, sprinkle with pepper, then cook over hot coals for about 8–10 minutes until just cooked through, turning once.
4 Spoon half the Tomato Sauce over the bottom of a large flat dish.
5 Remove the fish steaks from the barbecue and arrange in the dish in a single layer. Top with the remaining Tomato Sauce.
6 Either serve immediately, or allow the fish steaks to cool to room temperature and absorb the flavours of the sauce, then serve.

WHOLE FISH FROM THE GREEK ISLANDS

These fish are cooked whole on the barbecue, usually basted with olive oil and lemon. For a crisp skin, scrape off the scales with a serrated knife, working from tail to head, then brush the skin with olive oil. Serve with a Greek salad of feta cheese, tomatoes and olives.

INGREDIENTS

2 whole fish, such as red or grey mullet, red snapper or tilapia, about 1kg (2lb) each
juice of 2 lemons
salt and black pepper
125ml (4fl oz) olive oil
6 bay leaves, plus extra to garnish
1 tsp dried oregano, crumbled

PREPARATION

1 Light the barbecue or preheat a gas barbecue.
2 Score the fish diagonally at 5cm (2in) intervals with a sharp knife. Rub inside and out with half the lemon juice, salt and pepper, and 2 tablespoons of the olive oil. Place the bay leaves inside the fish and sprinkle inside and out with oregano.
3 Place the fish over the hot coals, preferably in a wire basket, and cook for 10–20 minutes on each side. For larger fish (over 1kg), cook for up to 25 minutes on each side.
4 Sprinkle the fish with the remaining olive oil and lemon and serve immediately with a Greek salad. Garnish with bay leaves.

PROVENÇAL FISH IN LEAF PARCELS

Wrapping fish in leaves is a favourite method of cooking in Provence. It protects against the heat, and allows the fish to absorb the aroma of the smoke and leaves. Serve with salad, or a bowl of Aïoli (see page 66).

INGREDIENTS

4 sea bass fillets, about 750g (1½lb)
4 garlic cloves, finely chopped
4 shallots, chopped
2 tbsp olive oil
juice of ½ lemon
2 tsp chopped fresh tarragon, or ½ tsp dried
grated zest of ¼ orange
salt and black pepper
20–24 vine leaves, enough to make 4 parcels; if using leaves preserved in brine, rinse well then pat dry with kitchen paper

PREPARATION

1 Place the fish in a shallow dish and sprinkle with the garlic, shallots, olive oil, lemon juice, tarragon, orange zest and a good sprinkling of salt and pepper. Leave to marinate for 15–30 minutes at room temperature.
2 Light the barbecue or preheat a gas barbecue.
3 Place each fish fillet on a vine leaf and wrap up well, using as many leaves as it takes to cover it completely (see page 154). If necessary, use string to hold the leaves in place.
4 Cook the fish parcels over medium-hot coals, preferably covered. It should take about 15–20 minutes for the fish to cook through, turning once. Do not allow them to overcook.
5 Serve immediately, letting each person unwrap his or her own parcel. Accompany with a salad of orange, tomato and onion slices, tossed with Classic Vinaigrette (see page 44), or with a bowl of Aïoli (see page 66).

MAYAN SWORDFISH COATED WITH ANNATTO & CHILLI

This traditional Mayan recipe, from the Caribbean shores of Mexico, is one of the most delightfully exotic dishes I know. A whole fish such as snapper, tilapia or bass may be used instead of fish steaks or fillets. Corn tortillas and Black Bean Salsa (see page 125) make delicious accompaniments.

INGREDIENTS

4 tbsp cooked annatto seeds (see page 100), plus 2 tbsp of the cooking liquid
2 garlic cloves, finely chopped
½ tsp coarse salt
Spicy Mexican Marinade (see page 32)
½ tsp crushed cinnamon
½ tsp ground cloves
4 swordfish steaks, or other fish fillets, about 750g (1½lb)
handful of bay leaves, to scent the barbecue
bay leaves and lemon wedges, to garnish

To serve
1 onion, chopped
1 avocado, diced
2–3 tbsp chopped fresh coriander
2 ripe tomatoes, diced
pickled chillies, diced

PREPARATION

1 Purée the annatto seeds and the liquid with the garlic and salt, then mix with the Spicy Mexican Marinade, adding the cinnamon and cloves.
2 Rub the annatto-spice mixture on both sides of the fish steaks. Place in a shallow dish and leave to marinate at room temperature for 30–60 minutes, or in the refrigerator for up to 3 hours.
3 Light the barbecue or preheat a gas barbecue.
4 If using dried bay leaves, soak them in cold water until softened. Place the bay leaves on the coals to produce fragrant smoke.
5 Remove the fish steaks from the marinade. Cook the steaks over medium-hot coals for about 5 minutes, until golden brown and cooked through on one side, then turn, using a large spatula or fish slice, and cook the other side.
6 Serve immediately, sprinkled with chopped onion, avocado, coriander, tomatoes and pickled chillies. Garnish with bay leaves and lemon wedges.

VARIATION

MAYAN FISH WITH TROPICAL FLAVOURS To serve, omit the diced vegetables. Drizzle cool coconut milk over the hot fish and serve with diced banana and tomato, and lime wedges.

Garlic

Annatto liquid

Annatto seeds

Swordfish steaks

Spicy Mexican
Marinade

Cinnamon

Ground cloves

Bay leaves

Coarse salt

SCALLOPS WITH GINGER COCONUT SAUCE

INGREDIENTS

500g (1lb) shelled scallops
2 spring onions, thinly sliced
2 tbsp coarsely chopped peanuts
1 tbsp chopped fresh mint
Ginger Coconut Sauce
125ml (4fl oz) sweet white wine, such as Muscat
125ml (4fl oz) fish or chicken stock
2 tsp chopped ginger root
5 shallots, chopped, or 1 onion, chopped
250ml (8fl oz) water
125g (4oz) block coconut cream, crumbled
large pinch of saffron, soaked in
2 tbsp hot water, or a pinch of turmeric
grated zest of ¼ lime
juice of ½ lime, or to taste

PREPARATION

1 To make the sauce, combine the wine, stock, ginger, shallots, water and coconut cream in a small pan and bring to the boil. Cook over high heat until the onion is cooked through and the sauce has thickened, about 6 minutes.
2 Add the saffron liquid and the lime zest, heat through, then season with lime juice to taste. Strain the mixture if you prefer a smooth sauce.
3 Light the barbecue or preheat a gas barbecue. Get 8 skewers ready – wooden skewers should be soaked in water for 30 minutes.
4 Thread the scallops on the skewers and cook over medium-hot coals, 2–3 minutes on each side for small scallops, 4–5 minutes for larger ones, until slightly firm and lightly charred. Serve immediately with the sauce and sprinkled with the spring onions, peanuts and mint.

SCALLOPS WITH WILD MUSHROOM SAUCE

Mushrooms and cream are luxurious partners for the even more luxurious scallop. I find that the sweet cream and the woody flavour of mushrooms enhance the sweetness of the scallop. Thread the scallops and the mushrooms on skewers so that they do not fall into the fire.

INGREDIENTS

2 tbsp butter
1 garlic clove, finely chopped
½ tsp chopped fresh rosemary
2 tsp chopped fresh parsley
juice of ¼ lemon
salt and black pepper
500g (1lb) shelled scallops
125g (4oz) mushrooms
Wild Mushroom Sauce (see page 126)

PREPARATION

1 Light the barbecue or preheat a gas barbecue. Get 8 skewers ready – wooden skewers should be soaked in water for 30 minutes.
2 Melt the butter in a small pan, but do not let it brown. Swirl the garlic, rosemary and parsley into the hot butter, then season with lemon juice, salt and pepper.
3 Brush the scallops with the flavoured butter.
4 Thread the mushrooms and scallops on skewers, so that they do not fall into the fire. Cook over medium-hot coals, 2–3 minutes on each side for small scallops, 4–5 minutes for larger ones.
5 Meanwhile, heat up the Wild Mushroom Sauce.
6 When the scallops are slightly firm and lightly charred and the mushrooms cooked through, serve immediately with the sauce.

MUSSEL BROCHETTES FROM THE COTE D'AZUR

Barbecuing mussels on the open fire is one of the most delicious ways to cook them. In this dish the light marinade of fennel-scented fresh tomato sauce adds moisture, while the streaky bacon bastes the mussels with its savoury juices.

INGREDIENTS

1.75–2.5 litres (3–4 pints) mussels, well scrubbed
2 garlic cloves, finely chopped
½ tsp fennel seeds, crushed or ground
¼ tsp herbes de Provence, or to taste
375g (12oz) canned chopped tomatoes
3 tbsp olive oil
1 tbsp mild vinegar, or to taste
4–6 tbsp toasted breadcrumbs
8 rashers streaky bacon

PREPARATION

1 Light the barbecue or preheat a gas barbecue. Get 8 skewers ready – wooden skewers should be soaked in cold water for 30 minutes.
2 Place the mussels over medium-low coals for 8–10 minutes, preferably covered, until they open. Shell them, discarding any that fail to open.
3 Purée the garlic with the fennel seeds. Add the herbs, tomatoes, olive oil and vinegar and purée again until fairly smooth. Spoon half the mixture over the mussels in a shallow dish and leave to marinate at room temperature for 30 minutes.
4 Remove the mussels from the sauce and dredge in breadcrumbs.
5 Using 1 rasher of bacon per skewer, alternate bacon and mussels, letting the bacon wind its way from one end of each skewer to the other, with breadcrumbed mussels in between.
6 Cook over hot coals, preferably covered, for 5–6 minutes or until the bacon is browned and the mussels are crispy. Serve immediately with the remaining sauce.

SARDINIAN LOBSTER WITH OLIVE OIL, LEMON & TOASTED CRUMBS

I enjoyed this wonderful dish on a beach in Sardinia. The lobster was bathed in olive oil, lemon and herbs, then sprinkled with crumbs and roasted over the fire.

INGREDIENTS

1 garlic clove, finely chopped
175ml (6fl oz) olive oil
juice of 2 lemons, or to taste
½–1 tsp herbes de Provence
salt and black pepper
2 lobsters, prepared and split (see page 154)
4–6 tbsp dry breadcrumbs
lettuce leaves and lemon slices, to garnish

PREPARATION

1 Light the barbecue or preheat a gas barbecue.
2 Combine the garlic with the olive oil, lemon juice and herbes de Provence and season to taste.
3 Gently loosen the meat in the lobster shells with a paring knife. Stir the olive oil mixture well, then drizzle about half over the lobster meat.
4 Pat the breadcrumbs over the lobsters and cook over medium-hot coals, covered, until the breadcrumbs are lightly browned and crisp.
5 Serve immediately, garnished with salad leaves and lemon slices, with the remaining olive oil mixture as a sauce for spooning over as desired.

VARIATION

THAI LOBSTER For a completely different flavour, omit the garlic, olive oil, lemon, herbs and breadcrumbs. Instead, combine the Thai Marinade (see page 16) with 125–175ml (4–6fl oz) coconut milk, or 30g (1oz) creamed coconut dissolved in 125ml (4fl oz) hot water. Spoon half this mixture over the lobster halves, then cook as above until the tops are lightly browned. Serve the remaining Thai mixture as a sauce with the cooked lobster.

Whole Fish from the Greek
Islands (see page 67)

Mussel Brochettes from the
Côte d'Azur (see page 71)

*Sardinian Lobster with
Olive Oil, Lemon &
Toasted Crumbs
(see page 71)*

Malaysian Chilli Prawns

A spicy marinade enhances the sweet flavour of prawns. Serve as an appetizer with lettuce and a sprinkling of spring onions, or with rice as a main course.

INGREDIENTS

2 tbsp chopped ginger root
4 garlic cloves, finely chopped
2 tbsp vegetable oil
75–90ml (2½–3fl oz) ketchup
3 tbsp vinegar (preferably fruit or mild)
3 tbsp soy sauce
3 tbsp sugar
1 tsp crushed dried red chillies, or to taste
½ tsp cayenne pepper, or to taste
¼–½ tsp Szechuan peppercorns, lightly toasted and crushed
½ tsp five-spice powder
2 tsp sesame oil
750g (1½lb) raw king prawns, peeled but with tails left on

PREPARATION

1 Mix together the ginger, garlic, oil, ketchup, vinegar, soy sauce, sugar, crushed chillies, cayenne pepper, Szechuan peppercorns, five-spice powder and sesame oil.
2 Place half the mixture with the prawns in a shallow dish and toss until well coated. Leave to marinate for 30–60 minutes at room temperature.
3 Light the barbecue or preheat a gas barbecue. Get 8 skewers ready – wooden skewers should be soaked in cold water for 30 minutes.
4 Thread the prawns on skewers and cook over hot coals, turning them once or twice, for 2–3 minutes on each side, or until they become opaque and pink.
5 Brush the hot prawns with the remaining marinade, and serve on a bed of lettuce, sprinkled with spring onions.

Chilli-citrus Prawn Skewers with Bacon & Mango Salad

These spicy skewers make an excellent appetizer.

INGREDIENTS

500g (1lb) raw peeled prawns
Spicy Mexican Marinade (see page 32)
250g (8oz) smoked streaky bacon
2 frisée lettuces, lightly dressed in oil and lime juice
2 mangoes, sliced
spring onions and fresh coriander, chopped, to garnish

PREPARATION

1 Toss the prawns in the marinade in a shallow dish, then leave to marinate for 30–60 minutes at room temperature.
2 Light the barbecue or preheat a gas barbecue. Get 8 skewers ready – wooden skewers should be soaked in cold water for 30 minutes.
3 Thread prawns on each skewer with a rasher of bacon, alternating the bacon with the prawns and letting the bacon wind its way from one end of the skewer to the other.
4 Cook over hot coals for 3–5 minutes, until the bacon is browned and the prawns are just opaque.
5 Serve immediately, on a bed of frisée tossed with sliced mango. Garnish with chopped spring onions and coriander leaves.

Oysters with Spinach Relish

While fresh oysters are almost unbeatable, the scent of smoke enhances their flesh in this extravagant dish.

INGREDIENTS

48 oysters in their shells
Spinach Relish
½ garlic clove, finely chopped
large pinch of fennel seeds
3 tbsp cooked, chopped, squeezed-dry spinach
1 tbsp chopped fresh tarragon
3 tbsp melted butter
juice of ¼ lemon, or to taste
salt and black pepper

PREPARATION

1 Light the barbecue or preheat a gas barbecue.
2 Purée the garlic with the fennel seeds, spinach and tarragon, then mix well with the melted butter. Add lemon juice, salt and pepper to taste.
3 Place the oysters on the grill over medium coals until they open, 8–10 minutes. Carefully remove from the heat, and serve with the Spinach Relish.

LOBSTER WITH ROASTED GARLIC & CORIANDER BUTTER

Garlicky butter sauce is good with whole lobsters and lobster tails; the latter are sold frozen raw, so that when you barbecue them they cook rather than just warm through, as whole lobsters do when they have been par-boiled. Serve the smoky-flavoured lobster with hot and spicy Chipotle Salsa (see page 77) and warm corn tortillas (easily heated on the barbecue) for lobster tacos.

INGREDIENTS

12 garlic cloves, roasted until lightly charred and soft
4 garlic cloves, finely chopped
6 tbsp chopped fresh coriander
½ green chilli, finely chopped, or to taste
juice of ½ lemon
200g (7oz) butter
salt, to taste
2 large lobsters, halved lengthways (see page 154) or 4 medium–large lobster tails

PREPARATION

1 Light the barbecue or preheat a gas barbecue.
2 Squeeze the soft garlic from the roasted cloves (see page 152), then purée with the chopped garlic, coriander, green chilli and lemon juice.
3 Melt the butter but do not let it brown. Add to the garlic mixture and mix well until smooth. Add salt to taste.
4 Spoon about half the butter sauce on to the cut lobster halves, or tails, making sure that the fragrant mixture gets into all the crevices.
5 Place the lobster over the hot coals, preferably covered, for 10–15 minutes until heated through and lightly golden in places. If using lobster tails, cook for 15–20 minutes until they turn bright red. If cooking uncovered, turn once to mark the top of the lobster lightly with grill marks. Keep the butter sauce warm on top of the barbecue.
6 Serve immediately, with the butter sauce for dipping, Chipotle Salsa (see page 77) and warm corn tortillas.

VARIATION

MONKFISH WITH ROASTED GARLIC & CORIANDER BUTTER Spread 1kg (2lb) monkfish tails with a little of the butter. Place the fish, rounded side up, on a grill over hot coals for a few minutes to sear, then turn. Spread the cooked side generously with the butter and cook for about 7 minutes, or until the fish is just cooked through and the topping has a light crust.

CHILLI-CITRUS SQUID

For ease of preparation, buy the squid ready cleaned. Alternatively, see page 154 for instructions on how to prepare squid. Leave the squid bodies whole, and include the tentacles.

INGREDIENTS

3 garlic cloves, finely chopped
3 kiwi fruit, peeled and mashed
2 clementines, peeled, diced and mashed
juice of ½ lime
large pinch of cumin seeds
½–1 green chilli, such as Thai or Scots bonnet, finely chopped
3 tbsp olive oil, plus extra for drizzling
salt, to taste
500g (1lb) small squid, cleaned (see page 154)
paprika, to taste
chopped fresh coriander, spring onion and wedges of lime, to garnish

PREPARATION

1 Purée the garlic, then place in a shallow dish with the kiwi fruit, clementines, lime juice, cumin seeds, chilli, olive oil and salt.
2 Add the squid, turn to coat and leave for 30–60 minutes. Do not leave longer or the squid will lose its firm texture.
3 Light the barbecue or preheat a gas barbecue.
4 Cook the squid over hot coals for 2–3 minutes on each side, until just opaque and lightly marked from the grill. Take care that the tentacles do not fall through the holes of the grill.
5 Serve immediately, sprinkled with paprika and drizzled with olive oil. Garnish with coriander, spring onion and lime wedges.

VARIATION

SQUID SALAD This makes an ideal hot-weather salad. Serve the squid on a bed of frisée lettuce tossed with Classic Vinaigrette (see page 44). Accompany with crusty bread.

SEAFOOD WITH MANGO-PEPPER RELISH

INGREDIENTS

75g (2½oz) butter
3 garlic cloves, finely chopped
1 tbsp thinly sliced ginger root
24 mussels, cooked and shelled (see page 71)
4 scallops, shelled
12 raw tiger prawns in their shells
1 crab, shell and claws cracked
4 squid, cleaned (see page 154) and cut into pieces
thin strips of lemon and lime zest, to garnish

Mango-pepper Relish
large pinch of salt
1 small onion, chopped
½ green chilli, such as Thai or Serrano, chopped
½ red pepper, roasted, peeled, deseeded and finely chopped
1 tbsp olive oil
1 large ripe, firm mango, peeled, stoned and diced
juice of 1 lime, or to taste
2 tbsp shredded fresh mint

PREPARATION

1 Light the barbecue or preheat a gas barbecue.
2 To make the relish, purée 2 garlic cloves with the salt, then add the onion and green chilli and purée again until it forms a paste.
3 Add the red pepper, olive oil and mango, then season to taste with lime juice. Sprinkle with mint and set aside.
4 Melt the butter in a small pan until it foams, but do not allow it to brown. Remove from the heat and stir in the remaining garlic and ginger. Set aside and keep warm.
5 Skewer the mussels, scallops and prawns or place in a wire basket so that they do not fall into the fire, then place with the crab and squid over medium-hot coals, preferably covered so that the smoke can flavour the flesh. Cook for about 4–5 minutes on each side.
6 Serve immediately, with the ginger-garlic butter and the Mango-pepper Relish. Garnish with thin strips of lemon and lime zest.

SPICY SEAFOOD SOUP WITH GREEN BEANS

The basis of this soup is a Mexican technique for creating complex flavours: heat a small amount of oil in a pan, then ladle in several spoonfuls of spicy salsa. The heat of the oil "fries" the spicy sauce, reducing it to a concentrated paste. When stock is added it produces a soup with a rich, full-bodied flavour.

INGREDIENTS

1 squid, cleaned (see page 154), including tentacles
125g (4oz) shelled scallops, halved if very large
10 raw tiger prawns in their shells
10–15 mussels, well scrubbed
10 clams or crab claws, well scrubbed
2 tbsp vegetable oil or olive oil
4–6 tbsp Chipotle Salsa (see right)
1 litre (1¼ pints) fish stock
1 small onion, peeled and
sliced crossways
½ tsp cumin seeds, or to taste
salt, to taste
60g (2oz) green beans, preferably haricots
verts, frozen or fresh
1 tbsp chopped fresh coriander
4 lime wedges, to garnish

PREPARATION

1 Light the barbecue or preheat a gas barbecue.
2 Skewer the squid, scallop and prawns or place in small wire baskets so that they do not fall into the fire. Cook the shellfish over medium-hot coals, preferably covered to give a smokier flavour, beginning with the mussels (about 10 minutes) and clams or crab claws (10 minutes), then adding the prawns (about 5 minutes), and finally the squid and scallops (about 3 minutes). Remove from the heat when the mussels and clams have opened and the prawns have turned pink. Discard any shellfish that fail to open.
3 Heat the oil in a large pan and, when smoking, add the salsa. Cook the salsa in the oil, letting it reduce in volume and concentrate in flavour. When it is little more than a thick paste, add the stock, onion, cumin seeds and salt. Bring to the boil, cook for 5 minutes to allow the flavours to blend, then add the green beans.
4 Meanwhile, cut the squid into rings or bite-sized pieces, then add it to the soup along with the rest of the cooked shellfish and heat through. The green beans should be just tender but still almost crisp and bright green in colour.
5 Serve immediately in bowls, sprinkled with coriander and garnished with wedges of lime.

GRILLED MUSSELS WITH CHIPOTLE SALSA

This makes a sumptuous appetizer; for a main dish, double the amount and serve a spicy rice or pasta alongside.

INGREDIENTS

1.25 litres (2 pints) mussels, well scrubbed
salt
Chipotle Salsa
4–5 ripe tomatoes, diced
1–2 dried Chipotle chillies, cut into small pieces
125ml (4fl oz) water
3 garlic cloves, finely chopped
salt, to taste
½ onion, finely chopped

PREPARATION

1 Light the barbecue or preheat a gas barbecue.
2 Meanwhile, make the Chipotle Salsa. Place the tomatoes, chipotle chillies and water in a small pan. Bring to the boil and cook over a high heat until the tomatoes are just cooked through and the chillies are softened, about 5–7 minutes. Remove from the heat.
3 Purée the garlic with a generous sprinkling of salt, then add the onion and purée again. A pestle and mortar is best for this process as it draws out the essential, fragrant oils much more efficiently, but a food processor will also do.
4 Strain the tomato-chilli mixture, reserving the liquid, and add to the raw onion-garlic mixture. Purée, then stir in the reserved liquid. Add salt to taste and set aside.
5 Place the mussels over medium-low coals and cook, preferably covered, until they open, about 8–10 minutes. Discard any that fail to open.
6 Serve the mussels in their shells, with the Chipotle Salsa for dipping.

POULTRY

Chicken, turkey and duck are most enticing cooked on the barbecue. Crisp-skinned and succulent, they slowly turn to a rich brown hue. The variety of flavours is enormous, from strongly spiced chilli mixtures to delicate buttery sauces. Poultry should never be overcooked, as it then becomes dry and tasteless. Test with a skewer, removing from the heat immediately the juices run clear.

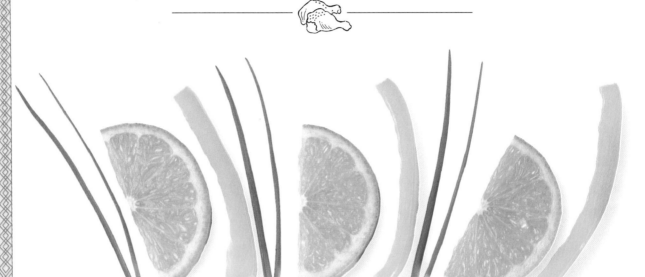

CHICKEN WITH GARLIC, LIME & TARRAGON

Make this a whole meal by cooking baby leeks and peppers alongside the chicken on the barbecue – I especially like a combination of yellow and green peppers, for colour as well as flavour. For a richer flavour, add a nugget of Tarragon Butter (see page 42) to melt on to the hot chicken.

INGREDIENTS

4 chicken quarters, about 300g (10oz) each
8–10 garlic cloves, finely chopped
4 lime quarters
salt and black pepper
4 tbsp dry white wine
90ml (3fl oz) olive oil
15g (½oz) fresh tarragon, chopped
8 baby leeks, trimmed
1 yellow pepper, cored, deseeded and cut into bite-sized chunks
1 green pepper, cored, deseeded and cut into bite-sized chunks
Tarragon Butter (see page 42), optional
15g (½oz) chives, chopped

PREPARATION

1 Place the chicken in a shallow dish and sprinkle with the garlic. Squeeze the lime quarters over the chicken, then cut into small pieces and add to the dish, along with the salt, pepper, wine, olive oil and half the tarragon. Leave to marinate for 2 hours or more. If marinating overnight, add only half the lime zest, as its oils can be quite strong.
2 Light the barbecue or preheat a gas barbecue.
3 Blanch the baby leeks for 1 minute in boiling salted water, then drain, rinse in cold water and drain again.
4 Remove the chicken from the marinade and pat dry. Brush the leeks and peppers with the marinade.
5 Place the chicken over hot coals to sear the skin, then move to a medium heat and grill slowly, turning occasionally, preferably covered, until cooked through and the juices run clear when pierced with a skewer, about 15–25 minutes.
6 Add the leeks 10 minutes before serving, then a few minutes later add the peppers. Cook until the vegetables are slightly browned and just tender. Serve the chicken with a nugget of Tarragon Butter, if liked, and sprinkle with the remaining tarragon and the chives.

BASQUE CHICKEN

Roasted, marinated peppers, combined with Pesto, make a zesty, easily prepared sauce for barbecued chicken.

INGREDIENTS

4 chicken quarters, about 300g (10oz) each
5 garlic cloves, finely chopped
2 tbsp white wine
salt and black pepper
4 tbsp Pesto (see page 124)
4 tbsp olive oil
1 green pepper, roasted, peeled, cored, deseeded
and cut into thin strips
1 red pepper, roasted, peeled, cored, deseeded
and cut into thin strips
2 tbsp white wine vinegar or balsamic vinegar

PREPARATION

1 Place the chicken in a shallow dish. Blend together 2 of the garlic cloves, the white wine, salt and pepper, half the Pesto and half the olive oil. Pour this marinade over the chicken, turn to coat and leave for at least 30 minutes at room temperature, or overnight in the refrigerator.
2 Combine the peppers with the vinegar and half the remaining garlic. Season to taste and leave to marinate for at least 30 minutes, or overnight.
3 Light the barbecue or preheat a gas barbecue.
4 Combine the remaining Pesto with the remaining garlic and olive oil and set aside.
5 Cook the chicken over medium-hot coals, beginning with legs and thighs. Cook for 10 minutes, turning occasionally, then add breast portions and continue until it is all cooked through and the juices run clear when pierced with a skewer, about another 10–15 minutes.
6 Combine the peppers with the Pesto mixture and serve spooned over the hot chicken.

CHICKEN WITH WATERCRESS SAUCE

Chicken tastes marvellous with this watercress sauce. Cook the sauce briefly, to preserve its delicate freshness.

INGREDIENTS

4 chicken quarters, about 300g (10oz) each
3 garlic cloves, finely chopped
juice of ¼ lemon
2 tbsp olive oil
Watercress Sauce
60g (2oz) butter
2 shallots, chopped
1 garlic clove, finely chopped
1 bunch watercress, washed, dried, and coarsely chopped
13oz (400g) crème fraîche
salt and black pepper
juice of ½ lemon, or to taste

PREPARATION

1 To make the sauce, melt the butter over a low heat, add the shallots and garlic and cook gently until softened but not brown. Add the watercress, stir for 1–2 minutes, then remove from the heat.
2 Stir in the crème fraîche, mix well, then season and add lemon juice. Blend in a food processor until smooth, then set aside to cool.
3 Place the chicken in a shallow dish, sprinkle with the garlic, lemon juice and olive oil, and season to taste. Marinate for at least an hour, or in the refrigerator for up to 2 days.
4 Light the barbecue or preheat a gas barbecue.
5 Cook legs and thighs over medium coals for 10 minutes, preferably covered, turning occasionally. Add the breasts and cook for another 10–15 minutes or until the juices run clear when pierced with a skewer. Warm the sauce and serve poured over the chicken.

CHICKEN WITH MUSTARD & GARLIC

INGREDIENTS

4 chicken quarters, about 300g (10oz) each
8 garlic cloves, thinly sliced
3 shallots, finely chopped
2–3 tbsp paprika
5 tbsp tarragon mustard or other mild mustard
3 tbsp strong Dijon mustard
3 tbsp olive oil
2 tbsp lemon juice
3 tbsp crème fraîche
salt and black pepper

PREPARATION

1 Place the chicken in a shallow dish. Mix the garlic, shallots, paprika, half the tarragon mustard, the Dijon mustard, oil and lemon juice in a bowl, add to the chicken and turn to coat. Cover and leave overnight in the refrigerator.
2 Light the barbecue or preheat a gas barbecue.
3 Grill legs and thighs over medium-hot coals for 10 minutes, turning once, then add the breasts and grill for 10–15 minutes, or until the juices run clear.
4 Mix the reserved mustard with the crème fraîche, spread over the hot chicken and season well. Serve immediately.

CHICKEN BREASTS STUFFED WITH MUSHROOMS

This dish was inspired by a damp, autumn forage for wild mushrooms. When the stuffed breasts are cooked quickly on the barbecue, the fragrance of the mushrooms permeates the flesh.

INGREDIENTS

6–8 dried or fresh morel mushrooms
6–8 ceps (porcini) or 6 slices dried ceps
4 boned chicken breasts, skinned
1 shallot, chopped
2 garlic cloves, finely chopped
2 tbsp olive oil
juice of ¼ lemon
salt and black pepper
Shallot Butter (see page 42), with 1 tbsp chopped red chilli added to the mixture
salad leaves and chives, to garnish

PREPARATION

1 If using dried mushrooms, pour boiling water over them, cover and leave for 30 minutes. Drain the mushrooms and squeeze out the excess liquid. Coarsely chop the mushrooms and set aside.
2 Cut a pocket lengthways in each chicken breast, then fill each pocket with a quarter of the mushrooms (see opposite). Secure with cocktail sticks, then arrange the breasts in a shallow dish.
3 Mix together the shallot, garlic, olive oil, lemon juice, salt and pepper. Pour over the chicken breasts and turn to coat well. Leave to marinate at room temperature for at least 1 hour.
4 Light the barbecue or preheat a gas barbecue.
5 Cook the chicken breasts over hot coals for about 4 minutes on each side, until they are just cooked through and the juices run clear when pierced with a skewer. Do not overcook.
6 Serve with slices of the Shallot Butter and garnish with salad leaves and chives.

CHICKEN BREASTS WITH PESTO

These tender morsels evoke the flavours of the Mediterranean. Serve with fresh pasta tossed with cream, Roquefort and pine nuts.

INGREDIENTS

4 boned chicken breasts, unskinned
2 tbsp white wine
2 tbsp olive oil
salt and black pepper
2 garlic cloves, finely chopped
2–3 tbsp Pesto (see page 124)

PREPARATION

1 Place the chicken breasts in a shallow dish and add the wine, olive oil, salt and pepper. Turn to coat, then leave to marinate for at least 1 hour.
2 Light the barbecue or preheat a gas barbecue.
3 Gently loosen the skin of each chicken breast down one side to make a pocket. Mix the garlic and Pesto and stuff a quarter into each pocket.
4 Cook over medium-hot coals until the chicken is just opaque, the skin is lightly marked from the grill, and the juices run clear when the flesh is pierced with a skewer, about 8 minutes. Serve immediately.

VARIATION

CHICKEN BREASTS WITH RED PESTO Combine 3–4 chopped sun-dried tomatoes, 1 chopped tomato and 2 tbsp Pesto. Stuff the chicken breasts as above.

CHICKEN WITH CHIVES & TARRAGON

The marinade gives a delightful yet unobtrusive sweetness to this chicken dish. I prefer to leave on the skin as it helps to retain the juices of the meat during cooking.

INGREDIENTS

4 boned chicken breasts, unskinned
Chive & Tarragon Marinade
3 tbsp muscat wine, such as Beaumes de Venise
3 tbsp olive oil
2 tbsp chopped chives
1 tbsp chopped fresh tarragon or ½ tsp dried tarragon
grated zest of ¼ orange
salt and black pepper

PREPARATION

1 Arrange the chicken breasts in a shallow dish. Mix together the marinade ingredients and pour over the chicken. Turn to coat, then leave to marinate at room temperature for 1–3 hours, or overnight in the refrigerator.
2 Light the barbecue or preheat a gas barbecue.
3 Cook the chicken breasts quickly over hot coals, turning once or twice, until the juices run clear when the flesh is pierced with a skewer. The white flesh should be just turning opaque, the skin striped with marks from the grill, about 8 minutes. Do not allow them to overcook.
4 Serve immediately, with rice and a green salad.

STUFFING CHICKEN BREASTS

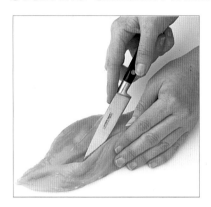

1 Using a sharp knife, cut a lengthways slit in each chicken breast, to form a pocket for the stuffing.

2 Carefully open out each pocket with the knife and fill with a quarter of the chopped mushrooms.

3 Secure the opening with a few cocktail sticks, to keep the stuffing in place while cooking.

Chicken Breasts Stuffed with Mushrooms

PAILLARDS OF CHICKEN WITH RASPBERRY-GARLIC BUTTER

A thin escalope of meat is called a paillard. Paillards can be duck, beef, veal, lamb or turkey, but these days are most often chicken. Because paillards are very thin they cook extremely quickly on the barbecue. The result is moist and tender.

INGREDIENTS

*2 chicken breasts, boned, skinned and halved
90ml (3fl oz) olive oil
3 garlic cloves, finely chopped
2 tbsp raspberry vinegar
4–6 sprigs fresh tarragon
salt and black pepper
Raspberry & Roasted Garlic Butter (see page 43)
handful of roasted garlic cloves (see page 152)
and fresh raspberries, to garnish*

PREPARATION

1 Place the chicken breasts between 2 sheets of waxed paper or clingfilm and gently beat flat with a rolling pin. Place in a shallow dish with the olive oil, garlic, raspberry vinegar, half the fresh tarragon, and salt and pepper to taste. Turn the paillards to coat well, then leave to marinate for 30 minutes–1½ hours.
2 Light the barbecue or preheat a gas barbecue.
3 Remove the paillards from the marinade and grill very quickly over hot coals, about 2 minutes on each side.
4 Place the paillards on individual plates and top with a slice of Raspberry & Roasted Garlic Butter to melt in. Garnish with a few roasted garlic cloves and raspberries, and the remaining tarragon.

VARIATION

HERBED CHICKEN PAILLARD WITH CORIANDER & GREEN CHILLI BUTTER Use white wine instead of vinegar in the marinade and add 3 tablespoons chopped coriander, 2 tablespoons chopped basil and 1 tablespoon chopped sage, marjoram or thyme. Serve the chicken with slices of Coriander & Green Chilli Butter (see page 42).

DOWN-HOME TEXAS BBQ CHICKEN

Barbecued chicken is a great favourite in Texas, where whole chickens are roasted over a fire to a crisp-skinned bronze. A spicy dry rub is the secret to the Texan flavour, and this one comes from Galveston. The Barbecue Sauce is not added before cooking: the long grilling would burn the sugar. Instead, brush some on during the last 5 minutes.

INGREDIENTS

*4 chicken quarters, about 300g (10oz) each
She-devil Barbecue Sauce (see page 127)*
Galveston Dry Rub
*1 tbsp salt
1 tbsp paprika
1 tbsp sugar
1 tbsp mustard powder
1½ tsp grated lemon zest
½ tsp cayenne pepper
½ tsp white pepper
½ tsp black pepper
1 tsp crumbled dried bay leaf
6 garlic cloves, finely chopped*

PREPARATION

1 Mix together the dry rub ingredients. Rub the mixture over the chicken pieces and leave for at least 1 hour, or overnight in the refrigerator.
2 Light the barbecue or preheat a gas barbecue.
3 Cook the legs and thighs over medium-hot coals for 10 minutes, turning occasionally. Add the breasts and cook for another 15 minutes, or until bronzed but not charred. Test with a skewer: the juices should run clear.
4 About 5 minutes before the end, brush with the Barbecue Sauce and cook until the chicken chars lightly. Serve with the remaining sauce.

VARIATION

BBQ BRISKET Cook a large brisket in stock until tender, then drain and marinate overnight in the Barbecue Sauce. Cook slowly over medium-low coals and serve sliced, coated with the sauce.

CARIBBEAN SPICY CHICKEN WINGS

Barbecuing is one of the best ways of preparing chicken wings. They turn out succulent yet crisp and make an excellent appetizer. Wings are also delicious with Szechuan Marinade (see page 86), or Teriyaki Marinade (see page 35).

INGREDIENTS

*1kg (2lb) chicken wings, wingtips removed and divided at the joint
Cajun Spice Rub (page 40)*
Caribbean Marinade
*juice of 2–3 lemons
1 onion, grated
6 garlic cloves, finely chopped
½ tsp ground cumin
1 tbsp syrup from a jar of preserved ginger
¼ tsp cinnamon
¼ tsp cayenne pepper
1 tbsp vegetable oil*

PREPARATION

1 Mix together the marinade ingredients in a large bowl. Add the chicken wings, toss to coat well, then leave to marinate for 1–3 hours at room temperature, or in the refrigerator overnight.
2 Light the barbecue or preheat a gas barbecue.
3 Remove the chicken wings from the marinade and dust with the Cajun Spice Rub.
4 Cook over a hot fire, turning once or twice until the wings are crisp and browned, about 15 minutes. Serve immediately.

AZERBAIJANI-STYLE KEBABS

Traditionally, these fragrant kebabs are served with mild onion slices, wedges of lemon or lime, a plate of fresh herbs such as tarragon, watercress, coriander, mint and chervil, and either soft or crisp flatbread.

INGREDIENTS

*4 boned, skinned chicken breasts or 500g (1lb) white turkey meat, cut into bite-sized pieces
3 tbsp melted butter*
Azerbaijani Marinade
*175g (6oz) natural yogurt
½ onion, finely chopped
5 garlic cloves, finely chopped
2 tsp paprika
¼–½ tsp saffron, dissolved in 1 tbsp warm water
5–6 tbsp chopped fresh mint
1 tsp salt
several generous shakes of Tabasco*

PREPARATION

1 Mix together the marinade ingredients.
2 Place the chicken in a shallow dish, add the marinade and toss well. Leave to marinate at room temperature for at least 3 hours, or in the refrigerator overnight or up to 2 days.
3 Light the barbecue or preheat a gas barbecue. Get 8 skewers ready – wooden skewers should be soaked in cold water for 30 minutes.
4 Thread the chicken pieces on the skewers, then place over a plate for a few minutes to allow the excess marinade to drip off.
5 Brush the kebabs with the melted butter and cook over hot coals, turning once or twice until the kebabs are lightly browned, about 5 minutes on each side, depending on the heat of the fire.

SKEWERS OF CHICKEN LIVERS, SAUSAGE & BACON

This makes an enticing party dish, served with a thick slice of ciabatta or French bread.

INGREDIENTS

*1 garlic clove, finely chopped
2 tbsp mild French mustard
1 tbsp chopped fresh rosemary
1 tsp chopped fresh parsley
90g (3oz) unsalted butter, softened
salt and black pepper
8 rashers smoked streaky bacon
4 Toulouse or Italian fennel sausages, cut into 2.5cm (1in) chunks
300g (10oz) chicken livers, cut into bite-sized pieces*

PREPARATION

1 Light the barbecue or preheat a gas barbecue. Get 8 skewers ready – wooden skewers should be soaked in cold water for 30 minutes.
2 Mix the garlic, mustard, rosemary and parsley with the softened butter, blending it well. Season and set aside.
3 Thread the bacon, sausage and chicken livers on to the skewers, allowing half a sausage and 1 rasher of bacon per skewer. Weave the bacon in and out of the sausage and livers, so that it bastes the livers while cooking.
4 Cook over hot coals, turning several times so that they cook evenly, about 5 minutes each side, or until the bacon is crisply browned, the sausage cooked through, and the livers still pink inside. During the last 2–3 minutes, slather a little of the butter on top of the kebabs. Serve hot, with the remaining butter spread on top to melt in.

SPATCHCOCKED POUSSINS WITH PROVENÇAL HERBS

*Restaurants in the hillside villages of Provence
specialize in dishes cooked over an open fire of scented
wood, then seasoned generously with local herbs.*

INGREDIENTS

*60g (2oz) unsalted butter
1½ tbsp flavoured wine vinegar, such as
rosemary or garlic (see pages 44–45)
4 garlic cloves, finely chopped
4 poussins, spatchcocked (see page 155)
salt and black pepper
2 tsp mixed dried herbs, including thyme, marjoram,
rosemary, fennel and savory
½ tsp dried crumbled bay leaves
15g (½oz) fresh basil leaves
fresh rosemary sprigs, to garnish*

PREPARATION

1 Gently heat half the butter in a small pan, then
add the vinegar and garlic. Cook for 1–2 minutes,
then remove from the heat.
2 Sprinkle the poussins with salt and pepper,
rubbing it in well, then brush all over with the
flavoured butter and sprinkle with dried herbs.
3 Loosen the skin in places along the breast and
thighs, making small pockets. Stuff a small nugget
of the remaining butter and a few leaves of basil
into each pocket. With a sharp knife make small
slits over the rest of the poussin and insert butter
and basil as before. Leave to marinate at room
temperature for 30–60 minutes.
4 Light the barbecue or preheat a gas barbecue.
5 Barbecue over medium-hot coals for 20–30
minutes until golden brown on the outside, but
still juicy inside, turning occasionally. The poussins
are cooked if the juices run clear when the thigh is
pierced with a skewer. Serve garnished with
rosemary sprigs.

VARIATION

MOROCCAN-FLAVOUR SPATCHCOCKED POUSSINS
Soften 60g (2oz) butter, then blend into it 8 finely
chopped garlic cloves, 2 tbsp chopped coriander, 6
finely chopped spring onions, 1 tbsp paprika, 1 tsp
ground cumin, salt and cayenne pepper to taste
and the juice of 1 lime. Rub this flavoured butter
all over the spatchcocked poussins, then leave for
at least 3–4 hours in the refrigerator to marinate.
Grill over medium-hot coals for 20–30 minutes,
turning several times, until the juices run clear
when the thigh is pierced with a skewer. Serve with
Tomato & Ginger Chutney (see page 128).

Garlic

Wine vinegar

Butter

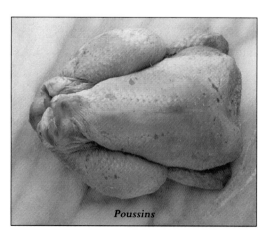

Poussins

Dried herbs

Bay leaves

Basil

Rosemary sprigs

Black
pepper

Salt

INDONESIAN POUSSIN

Throughout Indonesia, chicken, poussins, quail and birds of all kinds are marinated in spicy-sweet mixtures, then barbecued. You can smell them cooking over braziers set out on street stalls, where their aroma beckons irresistibly. Serve with steamed rice, crisp bean-sprouts and Cucumber, Carrot, Red Cabbage & Green Mango Salad (see page 134).

INGREDIENTS

4 poussins, spatchcocked (see page 155)
Indonesian Marinade (see page 36)

PREPARATION

1 Place the spatchcocked poussins in a large dish. Pour on the marinade. Leave for at least 3 hours at room temperature or overnight in the refrigerator.
2 Light the barbecue or preheat a gas barbecue.
3 Cook over hot coals, turning once or twice, until just cooked through, about 10–15 minutes on each side. Serve with steamed rice, crisp bean-sprouts and Cucumber, Carrot, Red Cabbage & Green Mango Salad (see page 134).

CHICKEN TIKKA

This kebab is traditionally prepared in a kiln-like tandoori oven. A covered barbecue works equally well, sealing in the juices and adding a smoky scent. Serve with Middle Eastern Spiced Pilaff (see page 133) and Cucumber-yogurt Relish (see page 129).

INGREDIENTS

4 boned, skinned chicken breasts, about 1kg (2lb),
cut into bite-sized pieces
juice of 1 lemon
30ml (1oz) butter, melted
Tikka Marinade
150g (5fl oz) natural yogurt
3 garlic cloves, finely chopped
2 tsp ground coriander
½ tsp turmeric
1½ tsp ground cumin
1½ tbsp paprika
¼ tsp ground ginger
large pinch of cayenne pepper
1 tbsp tamarind paste or mango chutney
To serve
salt
fresh mint leaves, chopped
fresh coriander leaves, chopped
½ cucumber, diced
lemon wedges

PREPARATION

1 Place the chicken pieces in a shallow dish, pour over the lemon juice and leave for 15–30 minutes.
2 Mix the marinade ingredients, pour over the chicken and turn to coat well. Leave for 3 hours at room temperature or overnight in the refrigerator.
3 Light the barbecue or preheat a gas barbecue. Get 8 skewers ready – wooden skewers should be soaked in cold water for 30 minutes.
4 Thread the chicken pieces on the skewers. Wipe with kitchen paper to remove the surface marinade, then brush with melted butter.
5 Cook over hot coals, preferably covered, turning several times, until the kebabs are just done, about 3 minutes on each side. Serve sprinkled with salt, chopped mint and coriander leaves and cucumber. Garnish with lemon wedges.

SZECHUAN CHICKEN & SHIITAKE MUSHROOMS

Serve with Chinese "crispy seaweed" – finely shredded green cabbage, deep-fried and drained on kitchen paper.

INGREDIENTS

4 chicken legs and 4 thighs, boned and cubed
4 spring onions, cut into 7cm (3in) lengths
250g (8oz) shiitake mushrooms
Szechuan Marinade
1 tsp Szechuan peppercorns, dry-toasted and ground
90ml (3fl oz) vegetable oil
3 tbsp rice wine or sherry
90ml (3fl oz) soy sauce
6 garlic cloves, finely chopped
1½ tsp five-spice powder
1 tbsp chopped ginger root
3 tbsp sugar
several generous shakes of Tabasco, to taste
grated zest of ½ orange

PREPARATION

1 Mix the marinade ingredients together.
2 Place the chicken, spring onions and mushrooms in a shallow dish, add the marinade and coat well. Leave for 3 hours at room temperature or 12–24 hours in the refrigerator, turning several times.
3 Light the barbecue or preheat a gas barbecue. Get 8 skewers ready – wooden skewers should be soaked in cold water for 30 minutes.
4 Thread the chicken, spring onions and mushrooms on the skewers. Cook over medium-hot coals for about 3 minutes on each side, until the chicken is browned and cooked. Serve with "crispy seaweed" scattered with toasted almonds.

CHICKEN WINGS SATAY

INGREDIENTS

1kg (2lb) chicken wings
6 garlic cloves, finely chopped
2 tbsp chopped ginger root
90–125g (3–4oz) sugar, or to taste
4 tbsp dry sherry or rice wine
125ml (4fl oz) dark soy sauce
2 tbsp sesame oil
6 spring onions
Indonesian Peanut Sauce (see page 124)

PREPARATION

1 Place the chicken, garlic, ginger, sugar, sherry, soy sauce and sesame oil in a shallow dish. Toss well, then marinate for at least 3 hours.
2 Light the barbecue or preheat a gas barbecue.
3 Grill the chicken over hot coals for about 15–20 minutes, or until browned and crisp, turning occasionally. Add the spring onions near the end of the cooking time. Serve with the sauce.

TURKEYBURGERS

INGREDIENTS

500g (1lb) minced turkey
1 onion, finely chopped
She-devil Barbecue Sauce (see page 127)
½ tsp ground cumin, or to taste
1 tbsp vegetable oil
salt and cayenne pepper, to taste

PREPARATION

1 Light the barbecue, or preheat a gas barbecue.
2 Mix the turkey with the onion, 3 tablespoons of sauce and the cumin. Shape into 4 patties.
3 Brush the patties with oil, then cook over hot coals for 3 minutes on each side. To serve, sprinkle with salt and cayenne, and brush with the remaining Barbecue Sauce.

BANGKOK-STYLE TURKEY WITH THAI DIPPING SAUCE

This spicy coconut marinade is also good with chicken, poussins, quail and the other poultry that appear skewered and barbecued on Bangkok's enticing food stalls. Steamed basmati rice and a green salad make the perfect accompaniments.

INGREDIENTS

1 turkey thigh, about 1kg (2lb), boned (see page 155)
and sliced into thin strips
1 courgette, sliced lengthways
1 red pepper, cored, deseeded and cut into strips
1 green pepper, cored, deseeded and cut into strips
Thai Dipping Sauce (see page 126), to serve
Bangkok Marinade
2 shallots, finely chopped
4 tbsp chopped fresh coriander
1½–2 tbsp chopped ginger root or galangal
4 garlic cloves, finely chopped
1 tsp diced lemon zest
juice of 1 lemon
3–4 tbsp soy sauce
300ml (½ pint) coconut milk, or 90–125g (3–4oz)
creamed coconut dissolved in 300ml (½ pint) water
4 tbsp sugar
1 red chilli, chopped, or to taste

PREPARATION

1 Mix together the marinade ingredients in a shallow dish. Add the turkey strips and toss well. Leave to marinate for at least 3 hours at room temperature or overnight in the refrigerator.
2 Light the barbecue or preheat a gas barbecue.
3 Just before cooking, toss the courgette and peppers in a little of the marinade.
4 Cook the turkey and vegetables over medium-hot coals, turning once or twice, until the vegetables become charred and tender and the turkey is cooked through, about 15–20 minutes. Serve with the Thai Dipping Sauce.

*Indonesian Peanut Sauce
(see page 124)*

*Szechuan Chicken & Shiitake
Mushrooms (see page 86)*

Chicken Wings Satay (see page 87)

Bangkok-style Turkey with Thai Dipping Sauce (see page 87)

TURKEY STEAKS WITH HUMMUS

This recipe is inspired by Middle Eastern dishes such as Circassian chicken. It is a tangy, refreshing dish, full of lightness and flavour. Serve with Rosemary Focaccia (see page 118) and a salad of ripe tomatoes.

INGREDIENTS

500g (1lb) turkey breast, cut into 4 steaks, about
5mm–1cm (¼–½ in) thick
2 garlic cloves, finely chopped
125g (4oz) hummus
2 tbsp olive oil
juice of ½ lemon
salt
hot pepper seasoning such as Tabasco, to taste
handful of rocket leaves
2 tbsp chopped fresh coriander
black olives, to garnish

PREPARATION

1 Light the barbecue or preheat a gas barbecue.
2 Place the turkey steaks in a shallow dish with the garlic and half the hummus. Turn to coat, then leave to marinate for 30–60 minutes.
3 Wipe the steaks dry with kitchen paper, then brush with olive oil. Cook quickly over medium-hot coals for about 3 minutes on each side, until the turkey is cooked through but still juicy.
4 Remove from the heat, then sprinkle the turkey with lemon juice, and season with salt and Tabasco to taste. Spread with the remaining hummus, top with rocket and coriander, and garnish with olives.

THANKSGIVING TURKEY

This serves 12–14. Accompany with Maple-roasted Sweet Potatoes (see page 58), Fire-baked Potatoes (see page 58), Fire-roasted Cherry Tomatoes (see page 53) and a relish (see pages 128-29).

INGREDIENTS

125g (4oz) butter, softened
1–2 tbsp chopped fresh sage
1 turkey, about 5.5–6.5kg (12–14lb)
salt and black pepper
1 onion, cut into chunks
2 celery sticks, cut into chunks
3 garlic bulbs
2–3 rosemary sprigs
½ bottle white wine, approximately

PREPARATION

1 Light the barbecue or preheat a gas barbecue.
2 Blend the butter with the sage then spread over the turkey, inside and out, and season. Place the onion, celery, garlic and rosemary inside the turkey and pour in 125ml (4fl oz) white wine. Secure the opening with a skewer.
3 Place a drip pan under the turkey and half-fill with wine. Cook, covered, over indirect heat (see page 147), allowing 12 minutes per 500g (1lb). When golden, test with a skewer in the thickest part of the thigh: the juices should run clear.
4 Leave the turkey to stand for 10 minutes then carve into portions. Skim the fat from the drip pan juices, boil to reduce slightly and pour over.

CHILLI-CHEESE STUFFED TURKEY BREASTS

These stuffed breasts are delicious and surprisingly simple to prepare. Serve with warm corn tortillas sprinkled with sliced spring onions and topped with sour cream. For a spicier dish, serve with a selection of salsas (see pages 124–25) and Tabasco.

INGREDIENTS

500g (1lb) turkey breast, sliced into 4 steaks
3 garlic cloves, finely chopped
1 fresh chilli, chopped
salt
3 tbsp chopped fresh coriander
150g (5oz) mozzarella or Fontina, cut into 4 slices
1–2 tsp cumin seeds
1 tbsp olive oil
2 ripe tomatoes, diced

PREPARATION

1 Light the barbecue or preheat a gas barbecue.
2 Place the turkey breasts between waxed paper or clingfilm, or inside a plastic bag. With a rolling pin or butcher's mallet, lightly pound the turkey to about half its thickness.
3 Sprinkle each escalope with garlic, chilli, salt and half the coriander, then cover one half of the escalope with a cheese slice, leaving a border round the edge. Fold over the escalope and press the edges together.
4 Sprinkle the top of the "parcels" with cumin seeds and drizzle olive oil over. Cook over medium-hot coals, turning after about 4 minutes to cook the other side. The cheese should be melted and the turkey just cooked through.
5 Serve immediately, sprinkled with the remaining coriander and the diced tomatoes, and salt to taste.

YUCATECAN TURKEY

*The sweet, garlicky, fruit and spice marinade
originates from the Caribbean shores of Mexico. The
turkey emerges from the barbecue richly flavoured,
meaty rather than poultry-like.*

INGREDIENTS

*1 turkey thigh, about 1kg (2lb), boned (see page 155)
and sliced into steaks 5mm (¼ in) thick*
Yucatecan Marinade
12 garlic cloves
125ml (4fl oz) pineapple juice
2 tbsp molasses sugar
juice of ½ lemon or lime
juice of ½ orange
*½ tsp each ground cinnamon, ground cloves
and dried thyme*
¼ tsp Tabasco, or to taste
½ tsp salt
¾ tsp black pepper

PREPARATION

1 To make the marinade, roast 10 garlic cloves,
unpeeled, in a dry pan for about 10 minutes until
slightly charred and softened. Allow to cool, then
squeeze out the flesh from the skins and mash (see
page 152). Chop the remaining garlic cloves.
2 Arrange the turkey steaks in a large shallow
dish. Mix the roasted garlic flesh and the chopped
garlic with the other marinade ingredients. Pour
the marinade over the turkey, turn to coat well
and leave to marinate at room temperature
for 2 hours.
3 Light the barbecue or preheat a gas barbecue.
4 Remove the turkey from the marinade and wipe
dry with kitchen paper. Cook over hot coals,
beginning with the skin-side down. Move the
steaks around on the grill, turning frequently so
that they cook evenly, about 15–20 minutes.
5 Serve the turkey steaks hot, with a spoonful
of Pickled Onion Rings (see page 129) and
another of Guava-apple Relish (see page 128).

DUCK WITH LAVENDER, THYME, HONEY & LEMON

*A classic Provençal dish. Serve with Fire-baked
Potatoes (see page 58) and roasted peaches.*

INGREDIENTS

*1 duck (giblets included), about 2kg (4lb), halved
2 onions, chopped
1 stock cube
1¾ pints (1 litre) water
15g (½oz) butter
3 tbsp brandy*
Provençal Marinade
*salt and black pepper
6 garlic cloves, finely chopped
3 shallots, chopped
1 tsp dried lavender, crushed
1 tsp thyme
½ tsp dried herbes de Provence or 2 tbsp
mixed fresh herbs
2 tbsp honey
1½ lemons, halved*

PREPARATION

1 To marinate the duck, sprinkle with salt and
pepper, half the garlic, the shallots, half the
lavender, the thyme, dried herbs and half the honey.
Squeeze the juice of 1 lemon over the duck and add
the lemon shells, cut into small pieces. Marinate
for at least 3 hours, or overnight in the refrigerator.
2 Meanwhile, place the duck giblets, half the
onion and the stock cube in a pan with the water.
Bring to the boil, skim, then simmer for 1 hour.
3 Light the barbecue or preheat a gas barbecue.
4 Remove the duck from the marinade and dry on
kitchen paper. Place a drip pan under the grill and
fill with about 7cm (3in) water or stock. Cook
over medium coals, covered if possible, for about
30 minutes, or until the duck is lightly browned
and glazed and the juices run clear if the flesh is
pierced with a skewer. Cut into portions and keep
warm. Skim the fat off the drip pan liquid.
5 To make the sauce, sauté the remaining onion in
butter until soft, then add the reserved garlic,
lavender and honey. Add the brandy, simmer for a
few minutes, then strain the hot stock and add a
ladleful. Boil to reduce, then add another ladleful.
6 Stir in the drip pan liquid. Continue to add
stock and reduce it 2–3 more times until the sauce
is concentrated in colour and flavour. Strain,
return to the pan and warm through. Add a
squeeze of lemon juice to the sauce then pour over
the duck and serve immediately, with Fire-baked
Potatoes (see page 58) and roasted peaches.

MANGO-MUSTARD GLAZED DUCK

*The spicy sweet hot glaze adds just the right accent to
this succulent dish. For a lean meat alternative
try rabbit: cook for the same length of time, brushing
with the glaze after the first 20 minutes.*

INGREDIENTS

*1 duck, about 2kg (4lb), cut into
halves or quarters
2 tbsp salt
1 tbsp sugar
black pepper
Mango-mustard Glaze (see page 41)*

PREPARATION

1 Place the duck in a shallow dish and sprinkle
with the salt, sugar and black pepper. Leave to
marinate at room temperature for at least 3 hours,
or overnight in the refrigerator.
2 Light the barbecue or preheat a gas barbecue.
3 Rinse the duck well, then dry on kitchen paper.
Place over medium-hot coals and cook slowly,
turning and moving the pieces frequently so that
the fat does not flare up and burn the flesh. Cook
the duck for about 20 minutes, or until the skin is
lightly golden.
4 Brush the glaze over the duck and continue
cooking for another 15–20 minutes, or until
glazed but not burnt. Serve immediately.

POMEGRANATE-CRANBERRY DUCK WITH SWEET BASIL

Duck is delectable marinated in tangy-sweet pomegranate syrup (grenadine) and wine, then grilled and served with a cranberry sauce. The sprigs of fresh basil, added at the last moment, perfume the dish with their sweet flavour and aroma. Serve the duck with Garlic & Spring Onion Mash (see page 133).

INGREDIENTS

1 duck, about 2kg (4lb), jointed and breasts cut in half
Pomegranate & Wine Marinade (see page 37)
handful of basil sprigs, to serve
Sauce
125ml (4fl oz) chicken or duck stock
125ml (4fl oz) red wine
125g (4oz) cranberries
1 tbsp sugar
2 shallots, chopped
salt and black pepper

PREPARATION

1 Place the duck pieces in a shallow dish and pour over the marinade. Turn until the duck is well coated, then cover and leave in the refrigerator for at least 12 hours.

2 Light the barbecue or preheat a gas barbecue.

3 Remove the duck pieces from the marinade and dry on kitchen paper. Cook slowly over medium coals, covered and over a drip pan if possible, for about 30 minutes, turning so that the fat is rendered out and the skin browns. Test the legs and thighs with a skewer: the juices should run clear.

4 Slice the breasts very thinly and keep the duck warm while you make the sauce.

5 Skim the fat off the drip pan liquid, if using. Combine the liquid with the stock, wine, 90g (3oz) of the cranberries, the sugar and shallots, and bring to the boil. Cook the sauce over high heat until it has reduced by half. Taste for seasoning.

6 Serve the duck with the sauce and the sprigs of basil. Garnish with the remaining cranberries.

MEAT

All meat seems to be at its best cooked on the barbecue: crusty on the outside, juicy and succulent within, scented with the smoke of the fire. Marinades and sauces enhance the possibilities, from simple wine marinades to pungent Central American jerks and rubs, and elaborate spicy concoctions from the Middle East.

BARBECUED HOISIN LAMB

Hoisin is one of the classic barbecue sauces of China. Sweet, tangy and spicy-hot, it is made from finely ground soy beans. For a vegetarian dish, serve the tofu on its own, surrounded by the grilled mushrooms, onions and aubergines. Accompany with bean-sprouts and steamed rice.

INGREDIENTS

8–12 fresh or dried shiitake mushrooms, stems removed
750g (1½lb) loin chops or lamb cutlets
285g (9½oz) tofu cake, cut into thick slices or fingers
about 12 x 7cm (5 x 3in)
Hoisin Marinade (see page 35)
1 tbsp soy sauce
1 tbsp sesame oil
2 onions, halved
4 small Asian or Japanese aubergines, sliced through
but left attached at the stem, then pressed open
to form fans
fresh coriander leaves, to garnish

PREPARATION

1 If using dried mushrooms, soak in warm water for 30 minutes, then drain and squeeze dry.
2 Place the lamb and tofu in a shallow dish, add half the marinade and turn to coat well. Leave for at least 4 hours at room temperature or in the refrigerator overnight.
3 Light the barbecue or preheat a gas barbecue.
4 Blend together the soy sauce and sesame oil. Brush the mushrooms, onions and aubergines with this mixture.
5 Cook the lamb, tofu and vegetables over hot coals. Each item should take 3–4 minutes on either side. As the various ingredients become tender and brown, move to a cooler part of the grill until they are all done.
6 When the chops are almost ready, brush with the remaining hoisin mixture. Serve the chops, tofu and vegetables with bean-sprouts and steamed rice and garnish with fresh coriander leaves.

PROVENÇAL LAMB

These tender lamb chops exude the flavour of the Mediterranean. I like to eat them with my fingers.

INGREDIENTS

750g–1kg (1½–2lb) loin chops or lamb cutlets
100g (3½oz) green olive paste (tapenade)
1½ tbsp herbes de Provence
2 tbsp olive oil
2 tbsp balsamic vinegar
5 garlic cloves, finely chopped
black pepper, to taste
15g (½oz) fresh basil leaves, thinly sliced or torn

PREPARATION

1 Place the lamb in a shallow dish with the olive paste, herbes de Provence, olive oil, vinegar, garlic and black pepper, and mix well. Leave to marinate for at least 2 hours.
2 Light the barbecue or preheat a gas barbecue.
3 Grill the chops over hot coals for 3–4 minutes on each side, depending on their thickness, so the meat is still rare. Serve sprinkled with basil.

LOIN CHOPS WITH GREEN MASALA

Serve these curry-scented little chops with Roasted Carrots (see page 53) and new potatoes.

INGREDIENTS

1kg (2lb) loin chops or lamb cutlets
Green Masala Marinade (see page 34)

PREPARATION

1 Place the lamb in a shallow dish with the marinade and turn to coat well. Leave for at least 3 hours, or overnight in the refrigerator.
2 Light the barbecue or preheat a gas barbecue.
3 Cook over hot coals for 3–4 minutes on each side, until crusty brown. Serve immediately.

BARBECUED LAMB NOISETTES

A red wine marinade enhances the flavour of lamb.

INGREDIENTS

4 medium or 8 small lamb noisettes
5 shallots, finely chopped
1 garlic clove, finely chopped
90ml (3fl oz) red wine
1–2 tsp dried tarragon or thyme
2 tbsp olive oil
salt and black pepper
lamb's lettuce, to garnish
Pink Peppercorn Butter Sauce
2 shallots, finely chopped
1 garlic clove, finely chopped
1½ tbsp pink peppercorns
1½ tbsp chopped fresh parsley
175g (6oz) softened butter
lemon juice, to taste

PREPARATION

1 Place the lamb in a shallow dish with the shallots, garlic, red wine and tarragon. Turn to coat well, then leave to marinate at room temperature for 30–60 minutes, or overnight in the refrigerator.

2 To make the Butter Sauce, mash the shallots, garlic, peppercorns and parsley into the softened butter and mix well. Add lemon juice to taste, to give a soft texture.

3 Light the barbecue or preheat a gas barbecue.

4 Remove the lamb from the marinade and rub well with olive oil.

5 Cook the noisettes quickly over hot coals for about 4–5 minutes on each side, until the meat is just cooked through, dark and crusty on the outside, and pink inside, or according to taste.

6 Sprinkle the noisettes with salt and pepper and serve with lamb's lettuce and a dollop of the Pink Peppercorn Butter Sauce.

ITALIAN BREAST OF LAMB

This recipe serves 6–8.

INGREDIENTS

*1.5kg (3lb) breast of lamb
2 garlic bulbs, cloves separated and finely chopped
3 tbsp dried mixed herbs
3 tbsp balsamic vinegar, plus extra for sprinkling
4 tbsp olive oil
salt and black pepper
1 fennel bulb, cut into bite-sized chunks, to garnish*

PREPARATION

1 Score the fatty side of the lamb, then rub the meat all over with garlic, herbs, vinegar and olive oil, and sprinkle generously with salt and pepper. Wrap well in clingfilm and leave to marinate for at least 3 hours, or overnight in the refrigerator.
2 Light the barbecue or preheat a gas barbecue.
3 Cook the lamb over low heat, preferably covered, for about 1–1½ hours, turning once or twice, until the meat is crisply browned on the outside and much of the fat has been rendered out.
4 Serve hot, sprinkled with balsamic vinegar and garnished with chunks of fennel.

MEAT PATTIES STUFFED WITH FETA

INGREDIENTS

*500g (1lb) lean minced lamb or beef
5 shallots, finely chopped
5 garlic cloves, finely chopped
90g (3oz) feta, sliced
salt and black pepper*
Crisp Salad
*½ cucumber, diced
1 red pepper, cored, deseeded and diced
2–3 handfuls of mâche, rocket or other greens
2 ripe tomatoes, diced
Classic Vinaigrette (see page 44)*

PREPARATION

1 Beat the minced meat in a bowl with the shallots and garlic. Form into 4 patties, then halve each one horizontally. Pat them out thinly. Cover 4 with slices of feta, then top with the other 4 halves. Pinch the edges to seal, then season.
2 Light the barbecue or preheat a gas barbecue.
3 Cook the patties over hot coals, preferably covered, for 3–4 minutes or until browned, then turn to cook the other side.
4 Toss the salad ingredients in a bowl. Top each patty with some salad and serve immediately.

BUTTERFLIED LEG OF LAMB

This is a classic technique: the boned leg of lamb is laid out flat so that it cooks evenly. Skewers help to keep the meat flat and easy to handle while cooking. It is important not to overcook the meat: serve it browned and slightly charred on the outside, pink and juicy inside. This recipe serves 6–8.

INGREDIENTS

*1 leg of lamb, about 2.5kg (5lb)
handful of rosemary sprigs
1½ garlic bulbs, cloves separated and cut into large slivers
250ml (8fl oz) red wine, plus extra if necessary
90ml (3fl oz) olive oil
salt and black pepper*

PREPARATION

1 Prepare the leg of lamb (see steps, right). Remove any remaining skin or excess fat and lay the boned lamb on a board, skin-side down.
2 Make 10–20 small incisions all over the meat with a sharp knife and insert a small sprig of rosemary and a sliver of garlic in each slit, using about half the rosemary and garlic. Lay the meat out flat in a large, shallow dish. Pour the red wine over the meat, then leave to marinate at room temperature for at least 1 hour.
3 Light the barbecue or preheat a gas barbecue.
4 Remove the meat from the marinade and wipe dry with kitchen paper. Use 4 long skewers to hold the meat flat in the "butterfly" position while it is cooking.
5 Finely chop the remaining rosemary and garlic, mix with the olive oil and brush half over the lamb. Season with salt and pepper.
6 Place a drip pan under the grill (see page 147) and pour in about 250ml (8fl oz) water. Place the skewered lamb on the grill and cook over hot coals for about 20 minutes on each side, covered if possible. Turn the meat from time to time and baste with the remaining olive oil mixture. The lamb is done when it is brown and charred on the outside, but still pink or rosy pink inside, according to taste. The total cooking time will be about 35–40 minutes.
7 Place the lamb on a board and leave to rest for about 10 minutes. Pour the liquid from the drip pan into a small pan. Skim off the fat and boil the liquid to reduce it if the gravy is thin. If the gravy is thick and concentrated, thin it down with a little wine.
8 Slice the lamb thinly and pour over the gravy. Serve with Red Onion and Raisin Relish (see page 128) and chargrilled green beans.

BUTTERFLYING LAMB

 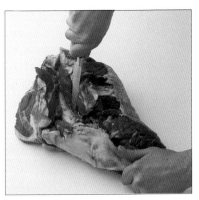 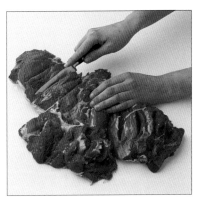

1 Cut round the shank (lower leg) bone with a sharp knife, then scrape the meat away from the bone until you expose the joint with the upper leg bone.

2 Continue to scrape the meat away from the leg bone. Sever the thread-like tendons and ease both bones out, cutting and scraping the meat away.

3 Open out the meat and make deep cuts in any thick portions so that it lies flat and is of even thickness all over. Remove any remaining tendons.

MOROCCAN LAMB BROCHETTES

This is consummate Moroccan street fare, cooked while you wait and best eaten immediately, while still hot. Serve with pieces of French bread and slices of tomato, and perhaps a salad of mixed herbs and olives.

INGREDIENTS

750g (1½lb) boneless chump chops,
cut into bite-sized pieces
1 onion, finely chopped
5 garlic cloves, finely chopped
2 tsp crumbled dried bay leaves or herbes de Provence
pinch of dried thyme
2 tsp ground cumin
½ tsp turmeric
juice of 1½ lemons
90ml (3fl oz) olive oil
salt and black pepper
1 tbsp paprika
1 tbsp chopped fresh coriander

PREPARATION

1 Place the lamb in a shallow dish with the onion, garlic, bay leaves or herbes de Provence, thyme, half the cumin, the turmeric, lemon juice and olive oil. Mix well, then marinate for at least 30 minutes and up to 3 hours at room temperature, or overnight in the refrigerator.
2 Light the barbecue or preheat a gas barbecue. Get 8 skewers ready – wooden skewers should be soaked in cold water for 30 minutes.
3 Thread the lamb on to skewers, then season to taste. Cook over hot coals until browned on one side, about 5 minutes, then turn and cook the other side. Be careful not to overcook.
4 Serve the kebabs immediately, sprinkled with the remaining cumin, the paprika and coriander.

FILLET OF BEEF

Cooking a whole or half fillet of beef is a rare treat, so long as it is not overdone. This is one of the most spectacular dishes I have barbecued, all the more remarkable for its simplicity. Serve with fettuccine tossed with crumbled Roquefort, crème fraîche, chopped shallots and pine nuts. This recipe serves 4–6.

INGREDIENTS

1–1.5kg (2–3lb) fillet of beef, fat trimmed
250ml (8fl oz) dry red wine
1 onion, chopped
2 garlic cloves, finely chopped
125ml (4fl oz) olive oil
salt and black pepper

PREPARATION

1 Place the beef fillet in a shallow dish with the wine, onion, garlic and half the olive oil. Turn to coat well, then leave to marinate at room temperature for up to 3 hours.
2 Light the barbecue or preheat a gas barbecue.
3 Remove the fillet from the marinade and rub well with the remaining olive oil.
4 Cook, preferably covered, until the meat is browned but still rare inside, or according to taste. Turn several times so that the fillet cooks evenly. It should take about 20 minutes and have a bit of "give" when pressed with the finger, but feel slightly firm. Test with a metal skewer to check that the colour of the juices is to your taste.
5 Remove the beef from the barbecue and leave to stand on a board for 10 minutes, to let the juices settle, before slicing. Serve sprinkled with salt and pepper, accompanied by fettuccine tossed with Roquefort, crème fraîche, shallots and pine nuts.

FAJITAS

Fajitas come from the border between Texas and Mexico. The name means "little belt" and refers to a specific cut of meat, skirt steak, though chicken and spicy sausages are often included in the dish. Fajitas are served with tortillas, Guacamole (see page 126), Salsa (see page 124), Refried Beans (see page 132) and sour cream.

INGREDIENTS

250g (8oz) skirt steak or other tender steak
Mexican Chilli Paste (see page 41)
4 tbsp tequila
1 chicken breast, boned but not skinned
2 chorizo sausages, poached, optional
3–4 small onions, unpeeled and halved lengthways
2 ripe plantains, peeled and halved lengthways
12 flour tortillas
1 red chilli, finely chopped
sliced limes, coriander and shredded lettuce, to garnish

PREPARATION

1 Spread the steak with half the chilli paste and leave to stand for 10 minutes. Sprinkle on 2 tablespoons of the tequila, then cover and marinate in the refrigerator overnight, or up to 2 days.
2 Spread the chicken breast with the rest of the chilli paste and sprinkle with the remaining tequila. Refrigerate for 1–2 hours.
3 Light the barbecue or preheat a gas barbecue.
4 Cook the steak over hot coals for 8–10 minutes, turning once or twice, until it is done on the outside and still rare inside, or to taste.
5 When the steak is half cooked, add the chicken and cook for about 4 minutes on each side, or until the juices run clear when pierced with a skewer. Do not overcook. Add the poached sausages, if using, onions and plantains, and grill for 2–3 minutes on each side.
6 Sprinkle each tortilla with a little cold water then heat for 30 seconds or so on each side. Keep warm in a clean tea towel. Alternatively, sprinkle the tortillas with a little water, then wrap in foil and place on the coolest part of the barbecue for about 5 minutes.
7 Remove the onions and plantains and place on a serving platter. Cut the steak and chicken into thin strips and slice the sausages. Arrange the meats on the platter and sprinkle with the chopped chilli. Serve with the tortillas, Guacamole (see page 126), Salsa (see page 124), Refried Beans (see page 132) and sour cream. Garnish with sliced limes, coriander leaves and shredded lettuce.

RATTLESNAKE JUNCTION BARBECUED STEAK

Cooked over an open fire, this is hearty fare from America's cowboy heartland. I like it best accompanied by thick slices of grilled onion and a tomato salad, with potatoes baked in the ashes. The zesty marinade is best used on tougher cuts of meat that need some tenderizing.

INGREDIENTS

1kg (2lb) rump, chuck or flank steak
Rattlesnake Junction Marinade
2 tbsp paprika
4 garlic cloves, finely chopped
125ml (4fl oz) beer
2 tbsp soy sauce
1 tsp dried thyme
2 tsp Dijon mustard
juice of ½ lemon

PREPARATION

1 To make the marinade, mix the paprika with the garlic, beer, soy sauce, thyme, mustard and lemon, then spread it over both sides of the steak.
2 Place the steak in a shallow dish and leave to marinate at room temperature for 3 hours, or covered in the refrigerator for up to 6 hours.
3 Light the barbecue or preheat a gas barbecue.
4 Cook the steak over hot coals, turning once or twice, until it is just cooked through, but not overcooked, about 8–10 minutes. It should be pink to red inside, to taste. Timing will vary according to thickness.
5 Serve sliced thinly across the grain. Accompany with thickly sliced barbecued onions, a tomato salad and baked potatoes.

STEAK JALISCO STYLE

This delicious steak is wonderfully simple: marinated in orange and olive oil and eaten rare, with a squeeze of lime and a sprinkling of cayenne.

INGREDIENTS

2 oranges, thinly sliced
4 tender beef steaks, such as sirloin or fillet,
250g (8oz) each
3 tbsp olive oil
salt and cayenne pepper
lime wedges and red chillies, to garnish

PREPARATION

1 Arrange half the orange slices in a shallow dish. Lay the steaks on top, then cover with the remaining orange slices. Drizzle with half the olive oil and leave for 1–3 hours.
2 Light the barbecue or preheat a gas barbecue.
3 Remove the steaks from the marinade and wipe dry. Rub lightly with olive oil, then cook quickly over hot coals for 8–10 minutes until just rare, or to taste, turning once or twice.
4 Sprinkle the steaks with salt and cayenne pepper and serve immediately, garnished with lime wedges and red chillies. Serve with Black Bean Salsa and Green Chilli Salsa (see page 125).

TUSCAN-STYLE STEAK

One of the glories of Tuscan cuisine, this steak dish is eaten drizzled with olive oil and lemon juice. Follow with ripe nectarines and a pungent cheese.

INGREDIENTS

4 tender beef steaks, such as sirloin or fillet,
250g (8oz) each
3–4 tbsp olive oil
pinch of dried sage or oregano
salt and black pepper
juice of 2 lemons

PREPARATION

1 Place the steaks in a shallow dish and pour over half the olive oil. Turn to coat, then sprinkle with the sage or oregano. Leave to marinate at room temperature for up to 3 hours.
2 Light the barbecue or preheat a gas barbecue.
3 Cook over hot coals for 8–10 minutes, until brown but still rare inside, turning once or twice.
4 Remove the steaks and sprinkle with salt and pepper, then drizzle with the remaining olive oil and lemon juice to taste. Serve immediately.

ANTICUCHOS

The national dish of Peru, anticuchos were traditionally made from llamas' hearts. Today, however, they are more likely to be prepared from beef heart or tender steak.

INGREDIENTS

1 tbsp annatto seeds
125ml (4fl oz) water
1 tbsp cumin seeds
4–5 garlic cloves, finely chopped
salt and black pepper
1 green or red chilli, chopped
175ml (6fl oz) red wine vinegar
2 tbsp olive oil
pinch of dried oregano or marjoram
750g (1½lb) sirloin or other tender steak,
cut into cubes
¼–½ tsp dried, crushed red chilli flakes
8–12 small hot red chillies, optional

PREPARATION

1 Place the annatto seeds and water in a small pan. Bring to the boil, simmer for 2–3 minutes, then remove from the heat and leave the seeds overnight to soften. Alternatively, omit cooking and soaking, and grind the seeds in a coffee grinder.
2 Toast the cumin seeds in a dry, heavy frying pan until fragrant, but not browned. Remove from the heat and crush in a pestle and mortar or grinder.
3 Purée the garlic with salt, then add the cumin, fresh chilli, black pepper, vinegar, 1 tablespoon of olive oil, and the oregano. Mix well.
4 Place the steak in a shallow dish, spoon over half the cumin-garlic mixture and turn to coat. Leave to marinate for 2–3 hours.
5 Light the barbecue or preheat a gas barbecue. Get 8 skewers ready – wooden skewers should be soaked in cold water for 30 minutes.
6 Drain the annatto seeds, reserving the cooking water. Crush the seeds, then stir in the cooking water, crushed red chilli and the remaining olive oil. If using ground seeds, add 90ml (3fl oz) water.
7 Heat the remaining marinade until it comes to the boil. Cook for 2–3 minutes, then remove from the heat and stir in the annatto mixture.
8 Thread the beef on to the skewers, adding 2–3 chillies if liked, then brush with some of the marinade-annatto mixture.
9 Cook over hot coals for about 8–10 minutes until browned, turning once or twice, then brush again with the mixture. Serve with chargrilled sweet potatoes and corn-on-the-cob, and a selection of relishes (see pages 128–29).

Georgian Shish Kebab

*Kebabs originated in the Caucasus, where legend has it
they were served up on the point of a sword – the
word kebab is actually Turkish. This style of cooking was
then taken up by the Russians and Georgians, who
prefer kebabs made from beef rather than lamb.*

INGREDIENTS

*750g (1½lb) sirloin or other beef, cut into
bite-sized cubes
3–5 garlic cloves, finely chopped
1 small onion, chopped
10 black peppercorns, coarsely ground
250ml (8fl oz) red wine
handful of fresh bay leaves
3 small onions, cut into wedges
3 green peppers, cored, deseeded and cut into wedges
125ml (4fl oz) sunflower oil
salt and black pepper
lemon slices and pickled, sweet red peppers, to garnish*

PREPARATION

1 Place the beef in a shallow dish with the garlic,
onion, peppercorns, wine and bay leaves. Turn to
coat, then leave to marinate for at least 3 hours
and up to 8 hours at room temperature, or
overnight in the refrigerator.

2 Light the barbecue or preheat a gas barbecue.
Get 8 skewers ready – wooden skewers should be
soaked in cold water for 30 minutes.

3 Thread the meat and bay leaves on to the
skewers, alternating with wedges of onion and
pepper. Push the pieces tightly together on the
skewers and brush with oil.

4 Cook over hot coals, turning occasionally and
basting with oil as needed. Allow 5–7 minutes
for rare kebabs, 9–10 minutes for medium-rare,
and 12–13 minutes for medium. Be careful not to
spoil the kebabs by overcooking.

5 Serve immediately, sprinkled with salt and
pepper and garnished with lemon slices and
pickled sweet red chilli peppers.

Steak Jalisco Style
(See page 100)

Jerked Pork Ribs
(See page 105)

*Roasted Green
Chilli Salsa
(See page 125)*

*Anticuchos
(See page 100)*

STEAK & MUSHROOMS WITH ROASTED GARLIC BUTTER

When you are ready to barbecue, slather some of the butter on to the steaks and set them on the hot grill. When they are ready, slightly charred on the outside, rare within, top with a little more of the butter to melt into a sauce. Accompany with tender, crisp haricots verts, and ripe cheese and fruit for dessert.

INGREDIENTS

4 sirloin or fillet steaks, 175–250g (6–8oz) each
250ml (8fl oz) red wine
4 large brown mushrooms or a selection of wild mushrooms, such as oyster, shiitake, morels, porcini, chanterelles
2 tbsp finely chopped fresh parsley
Roasted Garlic Butter
5 garlic cloves, finely chopped
¼ tsp salt
15 roasted garlic cloves, flesh squeezed out (see page 152)
175g (6oz) butter
salt and black pepper

PREPARATION

1 Place the steaks in a shallow dish, pour over the wine and leave to marinate for 1–3 hours at room temperature, turning occasionally.
2 Meanwhile, to make the butter, purée the raw garlic with the salt, then add the roasted garlic flesh and the butter and purée until it forms a smooth paste. Season with salt and pepper.
3 Light the barbecue or preheat a gas barbecue.
4 Remove the steaks from the wine; they will have absorbed much if not all of it. Wipe dry on kitchen paper and spread on both sides with a layer of the garlic butter. You should have half the butter left.
5 Cook over hot coals for 8–10 minutes, turning once or twice, until the outside is lightly charred and the inside is still rare, or to taste.
6 When the steaks are half cooked, thread the mushrooms on to skewers and spread with a little of the remaining butter. Place on the barbecue and cook for a few minutes on each side.
7 Serve the steaks and mushrooms spread with the rest of the garlic butter so it melts enticingly on top, and sprinkle with chopped parsley.

KOREAN BEEF OR LAMB

Both the beef ribs and the lamb are fatty enough to baste themselves as they cook slowly. Serve with bowls of steamed rice sprinkled with spring onions, and a side dish of pickled cucumbers.

INGREDIENTS

1kg (2lb) beef short ribs or breast of lamb
125ml (4fl oz) soy sauce
4 tbsp sherry or saké
2 tbsp sesame oil
2 spring onions, thinly sliced
2 tbsp sugar
¼ tsp cayenne pepper, or to taste
5 garlic cloves, finely chopped
2 tsp chopped ginger root
90g (3oz) toasted sesame seeds

PREPARATION

1 Place the meat in a shallow dish with the other ingredients. Turn to coat and leave, covered, to marinate for 1–3 days in the refrigerator.
2 Light the barbecue or preheat a gas barbecue.
3 Cook the meat, covered if possible, over indirect heat (see page 147), turning occasionally, until it is brown and tender, about 35 minutes. Serve immediately, with steamed rice sprinkled with spring onions, and pickled cucumbers.

STEAK ALLA MEXICANA

INGREDIENTS

4 corn tortillas
250g (8oz) mild white cheese, grated
4 small steaks such as sirloin, 125g (4oz) each
olive oil for brushing
salt and black pepper
Chipotle Salsa (see page 77)
1 tbsp chopped fresh coriander

PREPARATION

1 Sprinkle the tortillas with a layer of cheese.
2 Brush the steaks with olive oil, then sprinkle with salt and pepper.
3 Light the barbecue or preheat a gas barbecue.
4 Cook the steaks over hot coals, covered if possible, for 3 minutes, then turn. Add the tortillas and cook until the steaks are browned, but still rare, and the cheese has melted. A cover will keep the meat juicy and help the cheese to melt.
5 Place each steak on a cheese-topped tortilla, then spoon over Chipotle Salsa to cover the steak. Sprinkle with coriander and serve immediately.

CHAR SIU-STYLE PORK

INGREDIENTS

125ml (4fl oz) hoisin sauce
4 tbsp ketchup
2 tbsp soy sauce
¼ tsp crushed Szechuan peppercorns, toasted
¼ tsp five-spice powder
⅛ tsp ground cumin
2 tbsp honey
4 boneless pork chops, 175–250g (6–8oz) each
3 spring onions, thinly sliced
2 tbsp chopped cashew nuts, toasted

PREPARATION

1 Mix the hoisin, ketchup, soy sauce, Szechuan peppercorns, five-spice powder, cumin and half the honey in a shallow dish. Add the pork and turn until it is well coated. Leave to marinate for up to 3 hours at room temperature or in the refrigerator overnight.
2 Light the barbecue or preheat a gas barbecue.
3 Remove the meat from the marinade and drain. Drizzle on the remaining honey then barbecue over medium coals, turning once, until the chops are just cooked through, about 15 minutes.
4 Serve thinly sliced, sprinkled with spring onions and cashews.

GREEK PORK CHOPS

INGREDIENTS

1.5kg (3lb) pork chops or spare rib chops
1 onion, finely chopped
3 garlic cloves, chopped
125ml (4fl oz) lemon juice
125ml (4fl oz) olive oil
1 tsp dried oregano or mixed herbs
salt and black pepper
olives, parsley and lemon wedges, to garnish

PREPARATION

1 Place the pork in a shallow dish with the onion, garlic, lemon juice, olive oil, oregano, salt and pepper. Turn to coat, then leave to marinate for at least 3 hours at room temperature or in the refrigerator overnight.
2 Light the barbecue or preheat a gas barbecue.
3 Remove the meat from the marinade and drain. Cook over medium-hot coals for about 8 minutes, preferably covered, until browned on one side, then turn and cook the other side.
4 Serve hot, sprinkled with salt and pepper and garnished with olives, parsley and lemon wedges.

JERKED PORK RIBS

"Jerk" is the Caribbean term for a very hot, spicy marinade. Jerked meat, marinated and cooked over the fire, is sold in smart restaurants and ramshackle cafés alike throughout Jamaica.

INGREDIENTS

1kg (2lb) pork spare ribs
Caribbean Jerk
1 onion, finely chopped
2 tbsp lemon or lime juice
90ml (3fl oz) olive oil
1 green chilli, chopped
2 tbsp ground allspice
5 garlic cloves, finely chopped
½ tsp dried thyme
½ tsp crushed, dried red chillies
½ tsp freshly ground nutmeg
1 tsp chopped ginger root
salt and black pepper
4 tbsp rum
3 tbsp dark brown sugar
10–15 bay leaves

PREPARATION

1 Combine all the jerk ingredients in a shallow dish. Add the ribs and turn to coat, then cover and leave overnight to marinate in the refrigerator.
2 Light the barbecue or preheat a gas barbecue.
3 Drain the pork and place on the barbecue. Remove the bay leaves from the marinade and scatter around the pork.
4 Cook the ribs slowly, preferably covered, until they are cooked through, about 35–45 minutes, and are crusty and browned. Brush with oil occasionally if very lean. Serve immediately.

VARIATION

JERKED PORK WITH GUAVA-APPLE RELISH Instead of ribs, use a boneless cut of pork, cut into bite-sized chunks and threaded on skewers. Cook for 5 minutes on each side, or until crusty and brown, then serve with Guava-apple Relish (see page 128).

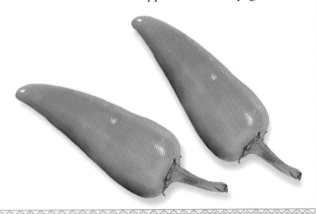

THAI-INSPIRED PORK

Make a double quantity of the spice paste for other uses: thinned with a little vinegar and sweetened with a bit more sugar, it makes a splendid dressing for thinly sliced cabbage, sweetcorn kernels and shredded carrots.

Sesame oil

Roasted peanuts

Ginger root

Lime juice

Brown sugar

Chicken stock

Sherry

INGREDIENTS

750g (1½lb) lean pork, cut into medallions
125ml (4fl oz) sherry, port or rice wine
125ml (4fl oz) chicken stock
2 tbsp brown sugar
2–3 tbsp lime juice

Thai Spice Paste
2 tbsp grated ginger root
2 tbsp medium sherry, port or rice wine
60g (2oz) roasted peanuts, chopped or coarsely crushed
4 spring onions, thinly sliced
1 tbsp each vegetable oil and sesame oil
1 green or red chilli, finely chopped
1½ tsp turmeric
1 tbsp brown sugar
1 tbsp balsamic or raspberry vinegar
2 tsp ground cumin
1 medium bunch fresh coriander, chopped
salt and black pepper

PREPARATION

1 Blend the Thai Spice ingredients together to make a paste (since the nuts are salty, you may not need any extra salt, depending on taste).
2 Rub about half the paste on the pork medallions and leave for 1–3 hours at room temperature or overnight in the refrigerator.
3 Remove the meat from the marinade with a slotted spoon. Place the marinade in a pan with the sherry, chicken stock, sugar and half the lime juice. Bring to the boil, then reduce the heat and cook until it forms an almost syrupy glaze.
4 Light the barbecue or preheat a gas barbecue.
5 Cook the pork over hot coals until charred on each side but juicy inside. Since medallions are so thin, this will take only 2–3 minutes on each side.
6 To serve, add the remaining spice paste to the sauce, along with the rest of the lime juice. Warm through and place a few spoonfuls on each plate with several slices of barbecued pork medallions on top. Serve with Middle-Eastern Pilaff wrapped in banana leaves (see pages 133 and 154) and Red Onion and Raisin Relish (see page 128).

VARIATION

THAI FILLET OF BEEF Coat thin slices of fillet with the Thai Spice Paste. Cook quickly over hot coals, so the meat is brown outside, but still rare inside.

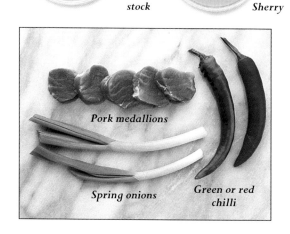

Pork medallions

Spring onions

Green or red chilli

Turmeric

Vegetable oil

Balsamic
vinegar

Ground
cumin

Coriander

Salt

Black
pepper

PORK & GINGERED FRUIT

Use pork that is already smoked, so it can safely be cooked with the sugary glaze, without fear of it burning.

INGREDIENTS

750g (1½lb) smoked pork loin, cut into chunks
Mango-mustard Glaze (see page 41)
30–45g (1–1½oz) softened butter
2 tbsp chopped, preserved ginger, plus some of the syrup
ground ginger or grated ginger root, to taste
½ pineapple, peeled, sliced and cut into chunks
2–4 ripe nectarines, stoned and cut into chunks
fresh mint sprigs, to garnish

Ginger Relish
4 tbsp chopped preserved ginger
3–4 dried apricots, diced
2 slices fresh pineapple, diced
2 tbsp chopped red chilli
1 tbsp chopped fresh mint

PREPARATION

1 Place the pork in a shallow dish with the Mango-mustard Glaze and turn to coat well. Leave to marinate for 30–60 minutes.

2 Light the barbecue or preheat a gas barbecue. Get 8 skewers ready – wooden skewers should be soaked in cold water for 30 minutes.

3 Mix the butter with the preserved ginger and syrup, and the ground or grated ginger. Spread the butter on the fruit.

4 Remove the pork from the marinade and thread the fruit and meat pieces alternately on to the skewers. Cook the kebabs over hot coals, preferably covered, turning once or twice until lightly browned round the edges, about 4 minutes on each side.

5 Mix together the Ginger Relish ingredients. Serve the kebabs immediately with the relish and garnish with mint sprigs. They are also good with steamed rice and a crisp vegetable salad.

BRINE-CURED PORK ROAST WITH PORT & APPLE SAUCE

Curing meat in brine firms it up and slightly pickles it (see page 155 for brining instructions). This recipe serves 6–8.

INGREDIENTS

2 tbsp fennel seeds
½ tsp dried lavender
2 tsp herbes de Provence
zest of 1 orange
Brine (see page 155)
1.5kg (3lb) boneless pork roast
olive oil, for rubbing
8 eating apples, cut into thick slices
250ml (8fl oz) meat stock
5–8 shallots, chopped
250ml (8fl oz) port, cider or apple juice
dash of raspberry vinegar, to taste
250g (8oz) crème fraîche

PREPARATION

1 Add the fennel seeds, lavender, herbes de Provence and orange zest to the other Brine ingredients and prepare (see page 155). Allow to cool then pour into a large glass bowl and add the pork. Cover and leave to steep in the refrigerator for 2 days.
2 Remove the meat from the Brine and rinse well in several changes of water. Dry the pork on kitchen paper, then rub well all over with olive oil.
3 Light the barbecue or preheat a gas barbecue. Place a drip pan under the grill and half-fill with water (see page 149).
4 Cook the pork, covered, over indirect heat with medium-hot coals for about 45 minutes, or until it is firm, cooked through and lightly browned.
5 During the last 10 minutes, place the apple slices over a cooler part of the fire and cook until warmed through and tender.
6 Place the meat on a platter to rest, with half the apples. Skim off the fat from the drip pan liquid.
7 Dice the remaining apples and place in a frying pan with the drip pan liquid, stock, shallots and port. Bring to the boil and cook over a high heat until reduced in volume by at least half.
8 Add the vinegar and any juices from the meat, boil for 1 minute then stir in the crème fraîche and cook over medium-hot coals for another 5 minutes, or until the sauce thickens slightly.
9 Slice the pork thinly and add to the frying pan, stirring gently, to warm through with the sauce and the sliced apples. Serve with rice and lamb's lettuce tossed in Classic Vinaigrette (see page 44).

BARBECUED VEAL CHOPS WITH WILD MUSHROOM SAUCE

This is a most luxurious dish, with a rich and elegant mushroom sauce.

INGREDIENTS

4 veal chops, preferably on the bone, 175–250g
(6–8oz) each
5 garlic cloves, finely chopped
2 tbsp olive oil
juice of 1 lemon
1 tbsp chopped fresh rosemary
Wild Mushroom Sauce (see page 126)
chopped chives, to garnish

PREPARATION

1 Place the chops in a shallow dish with half the garlic, the olive oil, lemon juice and rosemary. Leave to marinate for 1–3 hours at room temperature or overnight in the refrigerator.
2 Light the barbecue or preheat a gas barbecue.
3 Cook the veal over hot coals for about 6 minutes on each side, or until the outside is lightly charred but the inside is still pink.
4 Serve the chops with the Wild Mushroom Sauce poured over and sprinkled with chives.

POUNDED VEAL WITH ROSEMARY-MUSTARD BUTTER

Veal, delicate and bland, is enhanced by the same gentle flavourings as chicken breast.

INGREDIENTS

4 boneless veal cutlets cut from the leg,
about 175g (6oz) each
2 tbsp olive oil
juice of ½ lemon
salt and black pepper
Rosemary-mustard Butter (see page 42)

PREPARATION

1 Place the veal between 2 sheets of waxed paper or clingfilm or inside a plastic bag, and pound to 5mm (¼in) thickness.
2 Place the veal in a shallow dish with the olive oil, lemon juice, salt and pepper, and turn to coat well. Leave to marinate for 30–60 minutes.
3 Light the barbecue or preheat a gas barbecue.
4 Cook the cutlets quickly over hot coals for about 8 minutes, turning once or twice, until lightly charred but still pink inside. Spread with the flavoured butter and serve immediately.

FIRE-ROASTED RABBIT WITH PANCETTA, HERBS, OLIVADA & AÏOLI

Rabbit is delicious cooked over an open fire, but since it is so lean, care must be taken to baste it with oil and, of course, not to overcook it.

INGREDIENTS

3 tbsp olive oil
1 tbsp lemon juice
1–2 tsp herbes de Provence
4 garlic cloves, finely chopped
salt and black pepper
1 rabbit, cut into individual portions
6–8 slices of pancetta or bacon
2 tbsp fresh marjoram or oregano
4 tbsp black olive paste and Aïoli (see page 66)

PREPARATION

1 Mix together the olive oil, lemon juice, herbes de Provence, garlic and seasoning. Rub the rabbit pieces all over with the mixture. Leave to marinate for about an hour at room temperature.
2 Light the barbecue or preheat a gas barbecue.
3 Wrap the rabbit pieces in slices of pancetta, securing each piece with a bamboo skewer.
4 Cook over medium-hot coals for about 30–35 minutes, turning several times and basting with any remaining marinade.
5 Serve immediately, sprinkled with marjoram and accompanied by a bowl of olive paste and another of Aïoli.

VARIATION

ROSEMARY-MUSTARD AÏOLI Omit the olive paste. Add to the Aïoli 2–3 tablespoons chopped fresh rosemary and 1 tablespoon wholegrain mustard.

CUMBERLAND SAUSAGES WITH CRANBERRY MUSTARD

The visual appeal of the long coils of Cumberland sausage adds to the delight of this dish. If unavailable, use any kind of meaty, herbed sausage – turkey sausage is especially good with the cranberry mustard. Only the very best quality sausages are worth barbecuing. For other relishes see pages 128-29.

INGREDIENTS

2 Cumberland sausage coils, about 500g (1lb)
1–2 tbsp Dijon mustard
3 tbsp cranberry sauce
1–2 tsp sugar, or to taste
½–1 tsp red wine or Berry Vinegar (see page 45)

PREPARATION

1 Light the barbecue or preheat a gas barbecue.
2 Cook the sausages over medium coals for 6–8 minutes on each side, or until golden brown.
3 Meanwhile, stir the mustard into the cranberry sauce, then stir in the sugar and vinegar.
4 Serve the sausages sizzling hot with the cranberry mustard.

WHITE SAUSAGES WITH PRUNES

White sausages, such as Bratwurst, are delectable cooked on the fire. One of my recent favourites was truffle-scented boudin blanc, toted back from Paris.

INGREDIENTS

16 pitted prunes
500ml (16fl oz) scalding hot black tea
2 tbsp melted butter
4 white sausages, about 90g (3oz) each

PREPARATION

1 Steep the prunes in the tea until the tea has cooled and the prunes have plumped up, about 30 minutes.
2 Light the barbecue or preheat a gas barbecue. Get 4 skewers ready – wooden skewers should be soaked in cold water for 30 minutes.
3 Drain the prunes and thread on to the skewers. Brush with the melted butter and set aside.
4 Cook the sausages over medium-hot coals, turning occasionally, until cooked evenly to a light golden colour, about 15 minutes.
5 When the sausages are half-cooked, place the prunes on the barbecue and heat while the sausages finish cooking. Remove the prunes from the skewers and serve with the hot sausages.

SAUSAGE SELECTION

*As well as the usual pork or beef, try duck, game,
chicken, turkey, even seafood sausages. Different types
will have differing cooking times, depending on
thickness – cut into one to test.*

INGREDIENTS

*1 kg (2lb) assorted sausages, such as smoked kielbasa,
Toulouse, merguez, chorizo, Bratwurst
4 onions, peeled and halved
3 peppers, red, yellow and green, cored, deseeded
and halved
2 fennel bulbs, quartered lengthways
2–3 tbsp olive oil
juice of ½ lemon
salt and black pepper
thyme sprigs, to garnish*

PREPARATION

1 Light the barbecue or preheat a gas barbecue.
2 Cook the sausages over medium coals,
turning to cook evenly. Test from time to time.
3 Toss the vegetables with oil and lemon juice,
and season. Add to the grill with the sausages.
4 As the individual sausages and vegetables are
cooked through, remove and keep warm.
5 Serve with a selection of relishes (see pages
128–29) and garnish with thyme.

VARIATION

NEW YORK SAUSAGE SANDWICH Choose
smoked kielbasa, Knackwurst, spicy or Italian
sausages. Omit the yellow pepper, fennel and
thyme. When the onions and peppers are done,
cut into dice. Serve in hot crusty rolls with a
spoonful of an onion-pepper relish.

BREADS & SNACKS

Dough baked over a wood or charcoal fire traditionally makes bread with a crisp crust and smoky scent (the best boulangeries in France bake in wood-burning ovens). Large thick loaves do not fare well on the barbecue, but pizzas, and flat breads such as focaccia, tortillas and pitta, are delicious cooked over the fire. So are bread and cheese kebabs, and the flat, chick-pea crêpe known in Nice as *socca*.

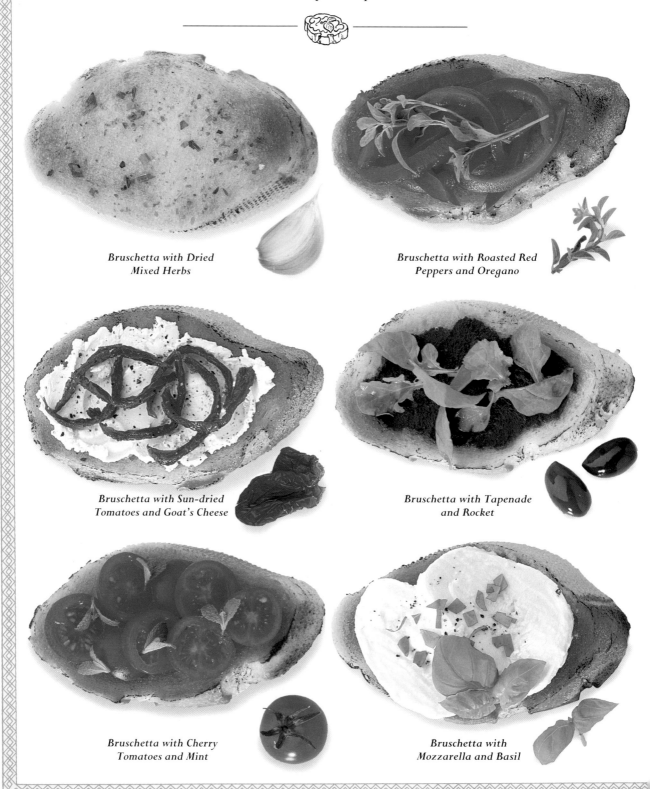

*Bruschetta with Dried
Mixed Herbs*

*Bruschetta with Roasted Red
Peppers and Oregano*

*Bruschetta with Sun-dried
Tomatoes and Goat's Cheese*

*Bruschetta with Tapenade
and Rocket*

*Bruschetta with Cherry
Tomatoes and Mint*

*Bruschetta with
Mozzarella and Basil*

BRUSCHETTA

*Bruschetta is delicious: what could surpass the pure
flavour of bread, toasted over the fire, rubbed
with garlic and anointed with rich olive oil. The
roughness of the toasted surface acts like a grater,
allowing the bread to pick up the strong
flavour and scent of the garlic.*

INGREDIENTS

*4 thick slices country bread, such as ciabatta
4 garlic cloves, halved
extra-virgin olive oil, to taste
salt, to taste, optional*

PREPARATION

1 Light the barbecue or preheat a gas barbecue.
2 Toast the bread slices on both sides over
medium-hot coals until crisp and golden.
3 Rub both sides of each slice with the cut garlic.
Drizzle with olive oil and serve. (If using
traditional saltless Tuscan bread, sprinkle with salt.)
TOPPING SUGGESTIONS Dried and fresh herbs,
roasted peppers, tomatoes, goat's cheese,
tapenade, rocket and mozzarella are all delicious.

ROSEMARY-GARLIC CIABATTA

*Crisped on the barbecue, this hot toasted bread makes
an excellent appetizer: serve with a plate of spicy
salami, fresh mozzarella, ripe garden tomatoes and
tangy green olives. It also makes a terrific
base for a hot melted sandwich.*

INGREDIENTS

*10 garlic cloves, chopped
salt, to taste
2–3 tbsp chopped fresh rosemary
125ml (4fl oz) olive oil
1 ciabatta, split in half,
then sliced into individual portions*

PREPARATION

1 Purée the garlic with salt, preferably in a pestle
and mortar, then add the rosemary and lightly
crush into the garlic mixture.
2 Mix in the olive oil, then brush most of this
mixture very generously on to the cut surfaces of
the ciabatta pieces.
3 Light the barbecue or preheat a gas barbecue.
4 Toast the bread on both sides over hot coals,
until crisp and golden brown.
5 Remove from the heat and brush once again
with the garlic-rosemary oil. Serve immediately.

BRUSCHETTA WITH SUN-DRIED TOMATOES & GOAT'S CHEESE

*This open sandwich can also be topped with a salad of
rocket leaves tossed in Classic Vinaigrette (see page 44).*

INGREDIENTS

*4 thick slices country bread, such as ciabatta
2 garlic cloves, halved
2 tbsp olive oil
125g (4oz) mild goat's cheese
8 sun-dried tomatoes, drained and sliced
black pepper*

PREPARATION

1 Light the barbecue or preheat a gas barbecue.
2 Toast the bread on both sides over medium-hot
coals until crisp and golden brown. Rub both sides
of the bread with the cut garlic.
3 Drizzle or brush each garlic toast on one side
with the olive oil, then spread with a layer of goat's
cheese. Arrange the strips of sun-dried tomato on
top. Sprinkle with black pepper and serve.

TOSTADAS IBIZA

*In a little hilltop village on the island of Ibiza
is a bar-café that specializes in these garlicky, toasted
cheese and ham sandwiches. The café is filled with the
sound of laughter and conversation, even passionate
arguing, while always in the background is
the call for just one more "tostada"!*

INGREDIENTS

*4 ciabatta rolls, cut open
60–90ml (2–3fl oz) olive oil
4 garlic cloves, halved
4 ripe tomatoes, halved
4 slices prosciutto, jamón or other ham
4 thin slices Manchego or Gouda
1 tsp dried mixed herbs*

PREPARATION

1 Light the barbecue or preheat a gas barbecue.
2 Brush the rolls generously with the olive oil and
toast the cut sides over hot coals until they are
golden brown and crunchy.
3 Rub the cut surface of each roll with the cut
garlic. Arrange the halved tomatoes on each roll,
then top with a slice each of ham and cheese.
Sprinkle a little mixed herbs on the filling, then
close the rolls.
4 Lightly toast the rolls on both sides until the
cheese melts, then serve immediately.

PIZZA DOUGH

I keep several batches of this dough in the freezer. Once it has defrosted, the pizza is very easy to put together.

INGREDIENTS

7g (⅓oz) dried easyblend yeast
425g (14oz) unbleached plain flour
3 tbsp wholewheat or rye flour
pinch of sugar
2 tsp salt
250ml (8fl oz) warm water
olive oil for oiling bowl and dough

PREPARATION

1 Mix together the yeast, 375g (12oz) of the plain flour, the wholewheat flour, sugar and salt in a large bowl.
2 Stir in the water and mix well, using a wooden spoon. When it forms a stiff dough, turn out on to a floured board. Knead well, sprinkling the dough with the remaining flour as you work to keep it from sticking. Knead the dough for about 5–8 minutes, or until it is elastic and smooth.
3 Place the dough in a large bowl coated with olive oil and rub oil over it. Cover with a clean cloth or clingfilm and leave in a warm, draught-free place until doubled in size, about 1½–2 hours.
4 Knock back the dough with your knuckles to expel the air. (At this point the dough can be placed in a plastic bag and frozen. When ready to use, defrost and proceed to step 5.)
5 Knead the dough lightly for 1–2 minutes, then return to the oiled bowl, cover and leave in a warm place to rise a second time, until it has again doubled in size, about 45 minutes.
6 Knock back the dough again, then roll or pat out on a large oiled baking sheet into 1 large pizza about 45cm (18in) across or 4 individual pizzas. Top as desired (see below), and bake over medium-hot coals. On an open barbecue the dough will need to be cooked on one side first (see page 116, step 3).

PIZZETTE WITH FIELD MUSHROOMS OR PORCINI

This makes 4 individual pizzas, slightly more elegant and less unwieldy than a large one. Smaller pizzas can be baked directly on the barbecue, as long as the grill is well oiled. If cooking on an open barbecue, see page 116.

INGREDIENTS

90g (3oz) dried or 175g (6oz) fresh ceps, porcini or other field mushrooms
1 quantity Pizza Dough (see left)
60g (2oz) tomato purée
2 garlic cloves, finely chopped
250g (8oz) mozzarella, thinly sliced
60g (2oz) freshly grated Parmesan or Pecorino
olive oil for drizzling

PREPARATION

1 Pour boiling water over the dried mushrooms, if using, and leave at room temperature for at least 30 minutes, or until softened. If using fresh mushrooms, simply slice them.
2 When the dried mushrooms are softened, drain and squeeze dry, reserving the soaking liquid. Cut off the hard stems.
3 Light the barbecue or preheat a gas barbecue.
4 Pat out the dough into 4 rounds. If cooking uncovered, see page 116, step 3 for instructions on pre-cooking the base, then continue as below.
5 Spread the tomato purée over each round of dough, then arrange the mushrooms on top. Sprinkle with garlic, then top with slices of mozzarella and a sprinkling of Parmesan or Pecorino. Drizzle with 2 teaspoons of the mushroom soaking liquid and with olive oil.
6 Bake the pizzas directly on the grill or on an oiled baking sheet over medium-hot coals, covered if using a covered barbecue.
7 Cook until the dough has puffed up and turned golden brown, and the cheese has melted, 10–15 minutes. Serve hot.

TOPPINGS FOR BARBECUED PIZZA

Most favourite pizza toppings are even more delicious on a barbecue-cooked pizza.

INGREDIENTS

grilled aubergine slices, roasted tomatoes and artichoke hearts; or
sun-dried tomatoes, basil and sweetcorn kernels; or
grilled radicchio, mozzarella and pine nuts; or
Pesto (see page 124); or
prosciutto and artichoke hearts; or
spicy lamb meatballs and mushrooms; or
roasted green peppers and ricotta; or
fresh herbs, prosciutto, garlic, and freshly grated Parmesan or Pecorino; or
sliced red onions, capers and sliced Fontina; or
a selection of barbecued vegetables (see page 10)

DOUBLE GARLIC PIZZA

There is a little restaurant in New York's Greenwich Village that is famous for its garlic pizza. For years, this has been my last stop before the airport; whether heading east to Europe or west to California, the infusion of garlic fortifies me for the rigours of the journey.

INGREDIENTS

1 quantity Pizza Dough (see page 114)
175ml (6fl oz) tomato passata
8–10 garlic cloves, finely chopped
2 tbsp chopped fresh parsley
large pinch of dried Italian herbs
250g (8oz) mozzarella, thinly sliced
freshly grated Parmesan or Pecorino
olive oil for drizzling
Garlic-oil Condiment
5–8 garlic cloves, finely chopped
4 tbsp olive oil

PREPARATION

1 Light the barbecue or preheat a gas barbecue.
2 Roll or pat out the dough on a large oiled baking sheet to make 1 large pizza about 45cm (18in) across. If cooking uncovered, see page 116, step 3 for instructions on pre-cooking the base, then continue as below.
3 Spread the top with tomato passata, then sprinkle with the garlic, parsley and herbs. Top with the mozzarella and grated Parmesan or Pecorino, and drizzle with olive oil.
4 Place the pizza over medium-hot coals and cover if using a covered barbecue. Cook until the dough has puffed up and turned golden brown, and the cheese has melted, about 10–15 minutes.
5 Meanwhile, make the Garlic-oil Condiment by combining the garlic and olive oil. For a mellow, less harsh flavour, heat gently until the first bubbles appear at the edge of the pan, then remove from the heat immediately.
6 Serve the pizza hot, drizzled with the garlic-flavoured oil.

VARIATION

When ripe sweet tomatoes are in season, they make a delicious and colourful topping. Place slices of tomato on top of the mozzarella, then sprinkle with the Parmesan or Pecorino. The tomatoes will roast as the pizza bakes.

ASPARAGUS PIZZA

From the moment I first tasted this, bought from a pizzeria in Florence one spring afternoon, it has been a favourite. It is simple to prepare and as comforting as it is lively. The Asparagus & Tomato Sauce should be prepared ahead of time, so that it is cool when spread on the dough.

INGREDIENTS

1 quantity Pizza Dough (see page 114)
handful of fresh basil leaves, thinly sliced
250g (8oz) mozzarella, thinly sliced
olive oil for drizzling
60g (2oz) freshly grated Parmesan or Pecorino, plus extra to serve
crushed dried red chillies, to taste
Asparagus & Tomato Sauce
2 tbsp olive oil
6 garlic cloves, finely chopped
500g (1lb) asparagus, ends trimmed and cut into bite-sized pieces
1kg (2lb) tomatoes, fresh or canned, chopped
salt and black pepper
sugar, to taste

PREPARATION

1 Light the barbecue or preheat a gas barbecue.
2 First make the sauce. Gently heat the olive oil in a pan, add the garlic and warm over low heat until its aroma is released but the garlic is not browned. Add the asparagus and cook for 2–3 minutes in the garlic oil.
3 Add the tomatoes, salt, pepper and sugar, and cook over a high heat until the tomatoes form a chunky sauce. Leave to cool.
4 Roll or pat out the dough on a large oiled baking sheet to make 1 large pizza about 45cm (18in) across or 4 individual pizzas. If cooking uncovered, see page 116, step 3 for instructions on pre-cooking the base, then continue as below.
5 Spread the top with the sauce, distributing the asparagus pieces evenly over the top of the pizza. Sprinkle with basil, arrange the mozzarella slices on top, then drizzle with olive oil and sprinkle with Parmesan or Pecorino.
6 Place the pizza over medium-hot coals and cover if using a covered barbecue. Individual pizzas can be baked directly on the oiled grill.
7 Cook until the dough has puffed up and turned golden brown, and the cheese has melted, about 10–15 minutes. Serve immediately, sprinkled with extra Parmesan cheese and crushed dried red chillies, to taste.

MEDITERRANEAN PIZZA

*Olive paste and a generous helping of garlic make
this pizza deliciously zesty. Serve with a green
salad tossed with Classic Vinaigrette (see page 44),
and a glass of Valpolicella or Zinfandel.*

INGREDIENTS

1 quantity Pizza Dough (see page 114)
150g (5oz) tomato purée
6 garlic cloves, finely chopped
3–4 tbsp cooked, chopped spinach, squeezed dry
75g (2½oz) black olive paste
4 black olives
1–2 tsp dried mixed herbs or thyme
4–5 sun-dried tomatoes in oil, diced, optional
200g (7oz) feta, thinly sliced
250g (8oz) mozzarella, shredded
2 tbsp olive oil

PREPARATION

1 Light the barbecue, or preheat a gas barbecue.
2 Roll or pat out the dough on a large oiled
baking sheet to make 1 large pizza about 45cm
(18in) in diameter. If using a covered barbecue
go to step 4.
3 If using an uncovered barbecue, you need to
cook the pizza base on one side first before adding
the topping. Place the pizza base on the baking
sheet over medium-hot coals and cook for 3–4
minutes, until the dough is lightly golden
underneath. Remove from the heat and turn the
pizza base over, so that the cooked side is
uppermost.
4 Spread the pizza with the tomato purée, then
sprinkle with the chopped garlic. Dot with the
cooked spinach and the olive paste, then sprinkle
with the olives, herbs and sun-dried tomatoes, if
using. Layer the feta and mozzarella on top, then
drizzle with the olive oil.
5 Place the pizza over medium-hot coals, cover if
using a covered barbecue, and cook until the
topping has melted and turned lightly golden in
places, and the dough has puffed up and turned
golden brown, about 10–15 minutes.

VARIATION

ARTICHOKE, SAUSAGE & OLIVE PIZZETTE Pat out
the dough into 4 individual rounds on an oiled
baking sheet. Follow step 4 above, but replace the
spinach with 2 artichoke hearts, sliced and
blanched, and add 2 continental pork or lamb
sausages, cut into bite-sized pieces. Arrange the
artichoke and sausage pieces on top of the cheese
before placing on the grill.

Black olives

Spinach

Garlic

Tomato purée

Pizza dough

Mixed
herbs

Sun-dried
tomatoes

Feta

Mozzarella

Olive oil

Olive paste

CRISP-CRUSTED FLAT BREADS

INGREDIENTS

500g (1lb) strong bread flour or plain flour
7g (⅓oz) dried easyblend yeast
1 tsp salt
2 tbsp vegetable or olive oil, plus extra
for oiling and drizzling
250–300ml (8–10fl oz) warm water

PREPARATION

1 Mix all the ingredients together in a bowl, using enough of the water to give a pliable dough, then turn on to a floured board and knead for 5 minutes or until the dough is smooth and elastic.
2 Place in an oiled bowl, cover and leave in a warm place for at least 1 hour, until the dough has doubled in size. Knock back the dough. (At this point it can be wrapped in clingfilm and frozen. When ready to use, defrost and proceed to step 3.)
3 Knead the dough lightly, then roll into balls the size of large eggs. Flatten the balls, then roll out into rounds 7–10cm (3–4in) in diameter and about 5mm (¼in) thick. Cover and leave in a warm place until doubled in size, about 40 minutes.
4 Light the barbecue or preheat a gas barbecue.
5 Place the rounds on the oiled grill over hot coals. Cover and bake for 5–8 minutes, or until the dough puffs up and turns golden brown.
6 Serve immediately with a Flavoured Butter (see pages 42–43) or drizzled with olive oil.

VARIATIONS

SWEET RAISIN FOCACCIA Knead 3 tablespoons of sugar and 2–3 handfuls of raisins or sultanas into the above dough. Roll out as directed, then sprinkle with sugar. Bake as above. Serve hot, with butter.
ROSEMARY FOCACCIA Knead 2–3 tablespoons of chopped rosemary into the dough. Rub with olive oil, roll out flat, sprinkle with coarse salt and bake as above. Serve with crushed garlic and olive oil.
FOCACCIA AUX LARDONS Knead 250g (8oz) of diced salt pork or bacon (lardons) into the dough. Roll out and bake as above.
HERB-PECAN FOCACCIA Roll out the dough as directed. Sprinkle with herbes de Provence, chopped fresh rosemary and 2–3 tablespoons of coarsely chopped pecans, then press into the dough with a rolling pin. Drizzle with olive oil and bake until lightly browned and puffed.
BULGARIAN CHEESE & ONION FLAT BREADS Knead 2 chopped onions and 250g (8oz) grated Cheddar into the dough. Roll out as directed, then press 175g (6oz) crumbled feta into the bread with a rolling pin. Bake until puffed and lightly golden.

SOCCA

Serve this Niçoise crêpe with Aïoli (see page 66).

INGREDIENTS

250g (8oz) chick-pea flour
1 tbsp coarse salt
500ml (16fl oz) water
pinch of herbes de Provence or thyme
olive oil for cooking

PREPARATION

1 Mix the chick-pea flour and salt then stir in half the water, stirring until the lumps dissolve. Add more water until the mixture has the consistency of single cream. Add the dried herbs.
2 Leave the mixture to stand for at least 30 minutes. Stir well before using.
3 Light the barbecue or preheat a gas barbecue.
4 Heat a crêpe pan over hot coals, then add 1–2 tablespoons of oil to coat the pan. Heat until smoking, then remove from the heat and pour in enough batter to form a layer 5mm (¼in) thick.
5 Cook over hot coals, preferably covered so that both sides cook at once, about 10 minutes. The edges should be brown, even a little scorched, and the top set rather than liquid, with brown spots.
6 Repeat with the remaining batter. Serve sliced.

QUESADILLAS

INGREDIENTS

4 green peppers, roasted, peeled, cored and sliced
(see page 54)
2 garlic cloves, finely chopped
1 hot green chilli, such as Jalapeño, chopped
salt and black pepper
3 tbsp olive oil
1 tbsp white wine vinegar
8 flour or corn tortillas
125g (4oz) goat's cheese, crumbled
125g (4oz) mozzarella, grated

PREPARATION

1 Slice the peppers, place in a bowl with the garlic, chilli, salt, pepper, 2 tablespoons of oil and the vinegar, and marinate for 30 minutes.
2 Light the barbecue or preheat a gas barbecue.
3 Brush the tortillas with the remaining oil and heat on the grill for 1–2 minutes.
4 Spoon peppers, goat's cheese and mozzarella on to each tortilla. Fold into half-moons. Cook over hot coals until the cheese has melted, 2–3 minutes. Serve hot.

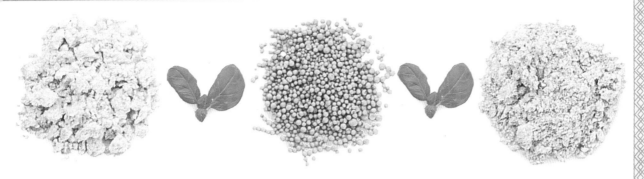

HALLOUMI, TOMATO & BAY LEAF KEBABS

*These make marvellous appetizers: full of flavour
and very fresh-tasting. Halloumi toughens as it cools,
so eat right away. See illustration on page 19.*

INGREDIENTS

*3–4 large tomatoes, each cut into 8 chunks
250g (8oz) Halloumi, cut into 24 chunks
3 garlic cloves, finely chopped
3 tbsp olive oil
24 bay leaves, preferably fresh*

PREPARATION

1 Light the barbecue or preheat a gas barbecue.
Get 8 skewers ready – wooden skewers should be
soaked in cold water for 30 minutes.
2 Place the tomatoes and Halloumi on a plate or
in a shallow dish. Sprinkle with garlic and olive oil,
then leave for 10–15 minutes.
3 Thread the tomatoes, Halloumi and bay leaves
on the skewers, allowing about 3 bay leaves, 3
chunks of cheese and 3 pieces of tomato per
skewer. Save any garlic and olive oil left on the
plate to season the hot barbecued kebabs.
4 Cook over hot coals for about 3 minutes on
each side, preferably covered. Serve immediately,
sprinkled with any leftover garlic and olive oil.

SPIEDINI

*These bread and cheese kebabs are traditional
to the region around Rome.*

INGREDIENTS

*175g (6oz) slightly stale French bread, cut into chunks
250g (8oz) mozzarella or Cheddar, cut into chunks
100g (3½oz) Pesto (see page 124)
1 garlic clove, finely chopped
3 tbsp olive oil
2 red peppers, roasted, peeled, cored and diced
(see page 54)
2 tbsp white wine vinegar*

PREPARATION

1 Light the barbecue or preheat a gas barbecue.
Get 8 skewers ready – wooden skewers should be
soaked in cold water for 30 minutes.
2 Thread the bread and cheese on to skewers,
starting and ending with bread. Push the bread
tightly on to the cheese so that it holds it in place.
3 Combine the Pesto with the garlic and olive oil.
4 Lay the skewers on a piece of foil and brush
lightly with a little of the Pesto mixture.
5 Place the foil over medium-hot coals, preferably
covered, so that the heat from the top toasts the
bread as it cooks.
6 Cook for about 8–10 minutes, turning if not
covered, until the bread is toasted and the cheese
has melted. Mix the remaining Pesto mixture with
the diced peppers and vinegar and serve with the
kebabs. If the cheese sticks to the foil, scrape it up
carefully and place it back on the Spiedini.

TOPINKA

*Topinka comes, I believe, from the Czech
Republic. Its main ingredients are rye bread and
garlic – the cheese can be varied at will.*

INGREDIENTS

*4 thick slices or 8 ordinary slices rye bread
4 garlic cloves, halved
125g (4oz) feta, thinly sliced
250g (8oz) white cheese such as
Cheddar, thinly sliced*

PREPARATION

1 Light the barbecue or preheat a gas barbecue.
2 Lightly toast the rye bread on one side over
the hot fire.
3 Rub the cut cloves of garlic over both sides of
the toasted bread. Place some feta on each piece of
toast, then top with a few slices of Cheddar.
4 Place the toast directly on the barbecue grill, or
on a baking sheet over the barbecue, and cook,
preferably covered, until the cheese melts.
Serve immediately.

FRUIT

Fruit is delicious on the barbecue, its natural sugars caramelizing with the heat of the flames. Because of its delicacy, a medium-low fire or the cooler part of the grill top is often the best way to barbecue most fruit. A slice of fruit, seasoned with whatever marinade the rest of the meal is seasoned with and cooked over coals, makes a perfect accompaniment to most meat, fish or poultry.

ROASTED BANANAS STUFFED WITH CHOCOLATE

Bananas are absolutely marvellous cooked on the barbecue, especially stuffed with chocolate! The chocolate melts as the bananas roast, and the result is an irresistibly gooey mixture. Serve with a dollop of whipped cream.

INGREDIENTS

4 medium-large ripe bananas, unpeeled
150g (5oz), about 24 squares, dairy chocolate
lightly whipped cream, if desired

PREPARATION

1 Light the barbecue or preheat a gas barbecue.
2 Slice through each banana lengthways with a sharp knife, cutting through the flesh but without cutting or tearing the bottom layer of skin. Stuff each banana with about 6 squares of chocolate and then wrap in foil.
3 Place the banana parcels over medium-hot coals and leave for about 10 minutes, long enough to melt the chocolate and lightly cook the bananas. They will be soft and slightly caramelized in texture and flavour.
4 Unwrap the foil from each banana and place in bowls, skin and all. Serve immediately, with a dollop of whipped cream if desired.

VARIATION

GRILLED RUM BANANAS Peel 4 medium-large ripe but still firm bananas. Sprinkle them with 2–3 tablespoons dark rum and with brown sugar and cinnamon to taste. Cook over medium-hot coals for 2–3 minutes on each side, making sure they do not overcook and become too soft. Serve immediately, with whipped cream or ice-cream.

ZESTY PINEAPPLE

This spiced fruit goes well with Eastern or Latin American flavours. Serve with Salsa (see page 124), crème fraîche and All-American Ribs (see pages 24–25); or with Chicken Wings Satay (see page 87).

INGREDIENTS

1 ripe pineapple, peeled and cored
2–3 tbsp light brown sugar, to taste
juice of ½ lime
½–1 tbsp crushed red chilli flakes, to taste

PREPARATION

1 Light the barbecue or preheat a gas barbecue.
2 Cut the pineapple into slices, then cut each slice into wedges. Place the pineapple in a shallow dish, add the sugar, lime juice and red chilli flakes and toss to coat well.
3 Cook over medium heat for 3–4 minutes on each side, until lightly glazed. Serve immediately.

ROASTED PEACHES WITH MASCARPONE & BASIL

INGREDIENTS

4 sweet, ripe but firm peaches, halved and stoned
2–3 tbsp melted butter
sugar, to taste
mascarpone, to taste
handful of fresh basil leaves

PREPARATION

1 Light the barbecue or preheat a gas barbecue.
2 Brush the peach halves with butter and sprinkle with sugar. Cook over medium coals for 2–3 minutes on each side. Serve immediately with a few spoonfuls of mascarpone, to taste, and some basil leaves.

HONEY-BASTED FIGS WITH RASPBERRIES & ICE-CREAM

Figs warmed on the grill and basted with a little honey and white wine make a sensuous and enticing dessert. The honey brings out the sweetness of the fruit, as does the heat of the grill. If ice-cream is not to your taste, fresh goat's cheese may be used instead.

INGREDIENTS

3–4 tbsp honey
1–2 tbsp dry white wine
12–16 ripe firm figs
600ml (1 pint) vanilla ice-cream
250g (8oz) raspberries

PREPARATION

1 Light the barbecue or preheat a gas barbecue.
2 Heat the honey and wine together, stirring until the honey completely dissolves into the wine. Remove from the heat.
3 Halve the figs and brush with the honey-wine mixture. If the figs are very small, use skewers or a piece of foil to prevent them falling through the bars of the grill.
4 Place the figs over medium-low coals (this is a perfect dish for using the last of the coals after cooking dinner). Cook for only a few minutes, brushing once or twice with the basting mixture.
5 Serve the hot figs in bowls with a scoop of ice-cream and some fresh raspberries.

S'MORES

For the uninitiated, S'mores are barbecued marshmallows, popped between biscuits with a square of chocolate. I hadn't thought of S'mores in years until recently in the South of France: my friends had just come back from the USA with this culinary souvenir. There in Provence we ate rosemary-scented lamb and aubergines. Then out came the marshmallows. The recipe allows for 2 each, but it all depends how greedy you are.

INGREDIENTS

8 marshmallows
16 wholemeal digestive biscuits
8 squares of chocolate

PREPARATION

1 Light the barbecue or preheat a gas barbecue.
2 Place the marshmallows on a stick or skewer and roast over hot coals until golden and flecked with brown. The traditional way to roast them is directly in the fire, but do not place on the cooking grill.
3 To assemble, place a hot marshmallow on a biscuit, top with a piece of chocolate and then another biscuit, sandwich-style.

HOT BARBECUED ORANGES WITH FRESH STRAWBERRIES

The orange slices should just warm through and lightly caramelize. Fresh fruit adds a sweet touch — raspberries or blueberries can be used instead of strawberries.

INGREDIENTS

4 oranges, peeled and sliced thickly
4 tbsp sugar
2 tbsp Curaçao or other orange-flavoured liqueur
250g (8oz) strawberries, hulled, sliced
and lightly sugared

PREPARATION

1 Light the barbecue or preheat a gas barbecue.
2 Toss the orange slices in a shallow dish with the sugar and liqueur. Leave the oranges to soak for about 15 minutes.
3 Place over medium-hot coals for 3–4 minutes, or until the oranges are lightly cooked and the sugar has caramelized. Serve immediately, topped with the sliced strawberries.

CURAÇAO FRUIT KEBABS

Serve sizzling hot — a bowl of vanilla ice-cream on the side makes a brilliant accompaniment.

INGREDIENTS

16 dried apricots (no-soak variety)
3 tbsp brandy
3 tbsp Curaçao or other orange-flavoured liqueur
2 ripe nectarines or peaches, cut into bite-sized pieces
½ ripe pineapple, peeled and cut into bite-sized pieces
2 large, just ripe bananas, peeled and
cut into bite-sized pieces
2 tbsp melted unsalted butter
3–4 tbsp sugar

PREPARATION

1 Light the barbecue or preheat a gas barbecue. Get 8 skewers ready — wooden skewers should be soaked in cold water for 30 minutes.
2 Place the apricots in a large shallow dish. Sprinkle over half the brandy and leave to soak for at least 30 minutes.
3 Add the liqueur, remaining brandy, nectarines, pineapple and bananas to the dish, and mix well.
4 Thread the fruit on the skewers, reserving the marinade. Brush the skewers with melted butter and sprinkle with sugar. Cook quickly over hot coals, allowing 3–4 minutes on each side. Serve with the marinade poured over the fruit.

LUSH FRUIT FEAST

INGREDIENTS

½ ripe pineapple, peeled and sliced, then slices halved
1 crisp apple, cored and sliced
1 pear, cored and halved
1 large firm ripe mango, peeled, stoned and halved
2 ripe firm apricots, stoned and halved
2 ripe firm nectarines or peaches, stoned and halved
2 ripe firm bananas, peeled and halved lengthways
4–8 ripe figs, whole or sliced lengthways
250g (8oz) black cherries, optional, pitted and threaded
on skewers or placed in a wire basket
sugar or honey, to taste
lemon or lime juice, to taste
white wine, rum or liqueur, to taste
melted butter, to taste

PREPARATION

1 Light the barbecue or preheat a gas barbecue.
2 Marinate each variety of fruit separately in 2–4 tablespoons sugar or honey, 1 tablespoon lemon juice and 3 tablespoons white wine or liqueur, to taste, depending on the sweetness of the fruit.
3 Cook the fruit gently over medium coals, basting with melted butter or honey. Remove the pieces of fruit as they become warmed and lightly glazed. Serve immediately.

VARIATION

FIRE & ICE FRUIT FEAST Barbecue a few fruits and pair each with an ice-cream or sorbet: for example, hot pineapple with pineapple sorbet; grilled cherries with sweet cherry ice-cream; sizzling hot bananas with cinnamon-flecked banana ice-cream.

SAUCES & ACCOMPANIMENTS

Barbecued foods need only the simplest of sauces to accentuate their strong flavours. Whether spicy, rich or tangy, sauces, salsas, chutneys and relishes will give finesse to the final dish. Choose from rice, polenta, vegetables and salads as an accompaniment.

PESTO

INGREDIENTS

3 garlic cloves, finely chopped
90–125g (3–4oz) fresh basil leaves, chopped
125ml (4fl oz) olive oil, or enough to make a thick paste
salt
60g (2oz) freshly grated Parmesan, optional
3–4 tbsp chopped pine nuts or walnuts, optional

PREPARATION

1 Purée the garlic, then add the basil and work into a fine mixture. Add the olive oil and purée again until it forms a thick sauce.
2 Season with salt, add the Parmesan and nuts, if using, and process until it forms a thick paste.
3 Store in a lidded jar, covered with a thin film of oil. It will keep in the refrigerator for up to 2 weeks, or in the freezer for up to 6 months.

RED CHILLI AÏOLI

A spicier version of the traditional Aïoli (see page 66).

INGREDIENTS

100g (3½oz) mayonnaise
1 garlic clove, finely chopped
1 tbsp mild red chilli powder or pure chilli powder
1 tbsp paprika
¼ tsp ground cumin
1 tbsp chopped fresh coriander
dash of lemon or lime juice
2–3 tbsp olive oil
salt and black pepper

PREPARATION

1 Combine the mayonnaise with the garlic, chilli powder, paprika, cumin, coriander and a dash of lemon juice.
2 With a whisk or fork, slowly mix in the olive oil, a little at a time, until it is absorbed. Season to taste and chill until ready to serve.

INDONESIAN PEANUT SAUCE

This keeps for 4–5 days in the refrigerator.

INGREDIENTS

4 garlic cloves, finely chopped
2 tsp chopped ginger root
150g (5oz) peanut butter
2 tbsp sugar
4 tbsp water
Tabasco, or other fiery chilli sauce, to taste
1 tbsp lemon juice
2 tbsp soy sauce
3 tbsp chopped fresh coriander
1 tbsp sesame oil
salt and black pepper

PREPARATION

Mix the garlic with the ginger, peanut butter and sugar. Slowly stir in the water, then when emulsified, add the Tabasco, lemon juice, soy sauce, coriander and sesame oil. Season to taste.

SALSA

This keeps for up to 1 week in the refrigerator.

INGREDIENTS

3–5 garlic cloves, finely chopped
1 small onion, chopped
1 tbsp chopped fresh parsley
1 tbsp chopped fresh coriander
10 ripe tomatoes or 400g (13oz) canned tomatoes, diced
1 tsp ground cumin
1–3 Jalapeño or Serrano chillies, finely chopped
1 tbsp lemon juice or vinegar
salt, to taste

PREPARATION

Combine the ingredients with a fork. Purée if you prefer a smooth salsa.

ROASTED GREEN CHILLI SALSA

INGREDIENTS

500g (1lb) Jalapeño or other medium-hot green chillies
2 tbsp olive oil
2 garlic cloves, finely chopped
salt and black pepper
juice of ½ lemon or lime

PREPARATION

1 Light the barbecue or preheat a gas barbecue.
2 Cook the chillies over hot coals until they are evenly charred on all sides. Remove from the barbecue and place in a plastic bag for at least 2 hours to steam off the skin.
3 Peel the roasted chillies, then remove the seeds and core. Chop finely and toss with the remaining ingredients.

MOJO ROJO

INGREDIENTS

1 dried medium-hot red chilli, such as Cayenne or Arbol
1 tsp cumin seeds
125ml (4fl oz) water
5–6 garlic cloves, finely chopped
2 tbsp paprika
125ml (4fl oz) olive oil
2 tbsp red wine vinegar
salt, to taste

PREPARATION

1 Bring the chilli, cumin seeds and water to the boil and cook over a high heat for about 5 minutes.
2 Purée the garlic, add the chilli mixture and paprika, then slowly blend in the olive oil. Add the vinegar and salt, and serve.

BLACK BEAN SALSA

INGREDIENTS

175g (6oz) canned black beans, drained
2–3 ripe tomatoes, diced
1 garlic clove, finely chopped
1 spring onion, finely chopped
1 red or green Thai or Serrano chilli, finely chopped
1 tbsp lime juice
¼ tsp ground cumin, or to taste
1–2 tbsp chopped fresh coriander leaves
salt, to taste

PREPARATION

Toss all the ingredients together, and serve.

MOJO VERDE

INGREDIENTS

5–6 garlic cloves, finely chopped
½ green pepper, deseeded and chopped
1 tsp cumin seeds
30g (1oz) chopped fresh coriander
125ml (4fl oz) olive oil
2 tbsp white wine vinegar
salt, to taste

PREPARATION

Purée the garlic with the green pepper, cumin and coriander. Slowly work in the olive oil, season with vinegar and salt, and serve.

Indonesian Peanut Sauce

Pesto

Red Chilli Aïoli

GUACAMOLE

The classic accompaniment to Fajitas (see illustration on page 26) and other Tex-Mex dishes.

INGREDIENTS

2 ripe avocados
½ onion, finely chopped
2 garlic cloves, finely chopped
2–3 tomatoes, diced
½ fresh green chilli, such as Jalapeño or Kenya,
finely chopped
juice of 1–2 limes
¼ tsp ground cumin
salt and cayenne pepper, to taste

PREPARATION

1 Cut the avocados in half and remove the stones. Scoop out the flesh and mash coarsely.
2 Combine the avocado with the remaining ingredients. Serve immediately, or cover tightly with clingfilm to prevent discoloration. (If the top does discolour, stir well just before serving.)

TEXAS JAILHOUSE BBQ SAUCE

I got this recipe from a Texas good ol' boy. He claimed that he had got it from his "great-grandpappy" who did a stint as a jailhouse cook.

INGREDIENTS

300ml (½ pint) ketchup
300ml (½ pint) beef stock
1 tsp mild chilli powder
1 tsp paprika
1 dried Chipotle chilli, crumbled
½ tsp dried mustard
pinch of ground ginger
3 garlic cloves, finely chopped
2–3 tbsp molasses sugar, or 1 tbsp molasses plus
1 tbsp brown sugar
1 tbsp Worcestershire sauce
salt and black pepper
1 tbsp lemon juice

PREPARATION

1 Combine all the ingredients in a small pan and bring to the boil. Reduce the heat and simmer for 10–15 minutes, or until the sauce has a smoky flavour and is well combined.
2 Allow to cool and serve at the table with barbecued steaks, chops, beef or pork ribs. The sauce can also be brushed on to food on the grill during the last 10–15 minutes of cooking time.

WILD MUSHROOM SAUCE

INGREDIENTS

30g (1oz) dried wild mushrooms, such as ceps or porcini
500ml (16fl oz) hot veal or chicken stock
5 shallots, finely chopped
2 garlic cloves, finely chopped
30g (1oz) butter
4 tbsp brandy
375g (12oz) crème fraîche
salt and black pepper
freshly ground nutmeg, to taste

PREPARATION

1 Place the dried mushrooms in a bowl and pour over the stock. Cover and leave for 30 minutes. When the mushrooms have softened, drain, squeeze dry and dice, reserving the liquid. Strain the soaking liquid (plus the squeezed liquid).
2 Sauté the shallots and garlic in the butter until softened and lightly coloured, then add the mushrooms and cook for a few minutes.
3 Pour the brandy into a long-handled ladle, then pour it into the pan, averting your face – it will spit. Boil until reduced to 2 tablespoons, then add the mushroom soaking liquid.
4 Reduce again over a high heat to about 175ml (6fl oz), then stir in the crème fraîche. Season to taste with salt, pepper and freshly ground nutmeg.

THAI DIPPING SAUCE

INGREDIENTS

7oz (200g) canned, chopped tomatoes,
juice included
2 tbsp dark brown sugar, or to taste
125g (4oz) sultanas, coarsely chopped
4 garlic cloves, finely chopped
½–1 dried red chilli, crumbled
½ tsp cayenne pepper, or to taste
3 tbsp cider or raspberry vinegar, or to taste
salt, to taste
3 tbsp water, plus extra if needed

PREPARATION

1 Combine the tomatoes with the sugar, sultanas, garlic, chilli, cayenne, vinegar and salt. Process until it is a slightly chunky mixture, adding water as needed to give the right consistency.
2 Bring the mixture to the boil in a small pan and cook for a few minutes to allow the flavours to mingle. Leave to cool.
3 Season with extra vinegar, cayenne, salt and sugar to taste.

SHE-DEVIL BARBECUE SAUCE

This sauce gets its kick from simmering the Chipotle chilli, a smoky dried chilli that harbours the heat of hell. It is an ideal sauce to brush on ribs towards the end of cooking.

INGREDIENTS

1 onion, coarsely grated
3–5 garlic cloves, finely chopped
4 tbsp Worcestershire sauce
250g (8oz) ketchup
4 tbsp molasses sugar
2–3 dried Chipotle chillies
275ml (9fl oz) beer, plus extra if needed
250ml (8fl oz) water, plus extra if needed
1 tsp dry mustard
1 tsp mild red chilli powder
1 tsp ground cumin
salt and black pepper
4 tbsp cider vinegar

PREPARATION

1 Mix together the onion, garlic, Worcestershire sauce, ketchup, molasses sugar, Chipotle chillies, beer, water, mustard, chilli powder, cumin, salt and pepper, and half the vinegar.

2 Bring to the boil, then reduce the heat and simmer for 30–45 minutes, or until it forms a thick sauce. If the mixture sticks or threatens to burn, add more water or beer.

3 When the sauce is thick and flavourful, add the remaining vinegar and taste for seasoning. Remove from the heat.

4 Slather this spicy, smoky sauce on ribs or steaks when they have almost finished cooking. Serve the remainder in a bowl for guests to help themselves.

Mustard

Chilli powder

Ground cumin

Salt

Black pepper

Cider vinegar

Beer

Chipotle chillies

Molasses sugar

Worcestershire sauce

Ketchup

Garlic

Onion

RED ONION & RAISIN RELISH

The relish is an excellent accompaniment to barbecued meats (see illustration on page 97). It will keep for up to 3 days in the refrigerator.

INGREDIENTS

3 large red onions, thinly sliced
125ml (4fl oz) olive oil
3–4 tbsp dark brown sugar
90g (3oz) raisins or dried cranberries
125ml (4fl oz) raspberry or cider vinegar,
or to taste
salt

PREPARATION

1 Cover the sliced onions with cold water and leave for 1 hour. Drain and dry on kitchen paper.
2 Heat the olive oil and sugar, stirring until the sugar dissolves. Add the onions and simmer until they go limp, about 15–20 minutes.
3 Stir in the raisins and vinegar. Continue to simmer until most of the liquid has evaporated and the onions are soft and melting. Season with salt and a dash more vinegar if needed.

TOMATO & GINGER CHUTNEY

This chutney is the ideal accompaniment for barbecued fish.

INGREDIENTS

1 small onion, chopped
2 garlic cloves, coarsely chopped
15g (½oz) butter
1 tsp chopped ginger root
pinch of ground ginger
1 green Jalapeño, Kenya or Serrano chilli, chopped
pinch of ground coriander
4 ripe tomatoes, diced
1–2 tsp sugar
salt, to taste
dash of vinegar, to taste

PREPARATION

1 Sauté the onion and garlic in the butter until softened, then add the ginger root, ground ginger, chilli and coriander.
2 Stir for a few minutes to blend the flavours, then add the tomatoes and sugar and cook over a medium-high heat for 3–5 minutes, or until it forms a sauce.
3 Season the chutney to taste with salt and vinegar. Serve at room temperature.

BEETROOT CHUTNEY

INGREDIENTS

140g (4½oz) pickled beetroot, diced
1 onion, diced
3 garlic cloves, coarsely chopped
2 tomatoes, diced
125g (4oz) sugar
½ tsp salt
½ Scots bonnet or other hot chilli, chopped
1 tsp dried mint
4 tbsp red wine vinegar
2 tbsp currants
1 tbsp tamarind paste
½ tsp ground coriander
1 tsp curry powder
juice of ½ lemon

PREPARATION

1 Place the vegetables, sugar, salt, chilli, mint, vinegar and currants in a small pan.
2 Bring to the boil, then lower the heat and simmer until the liquid is nearly evaporated and the vegetables have become almost jam-like.
3 Stir in the tamarind paste, coriander, curry powder and lemon juice, and remove from the heat. Serve at room temperature.

THAI GREEN MANGO RELISH

INGREDIENTS

1 green mango, slightly under-ripe, peeled and diced
1 tbsp sugar, or to taste
¼ tsp salt, or to taste
½ small red Thai chilli, very thinly sliced
½ small green Thai chilli, very thinly sliced

PREPARATION

Toss the diced mango with the sugar, salt and chillies. Serve with grilled fish or kebabs.

GUAVA-APPLE RELISH

INGREDIENTS

2 guavas, peeled and diced
1 small apple, peeled, cored and diced
dash of lemon juice, to taste
pinch of sugar, to taste

PREPARATION

Combine all the ingredients and chill until ready to serve.

CUCUMBER-YOGURT RELISH

See illustration on pages 130–31.

INGREDIENTS

250g (8oz) yogurt
½ cucumber, finely diced
2–3 garlic cloves, finely chopped
2 tbsp chopped fresh coriander or parsley
2 tsp chopped fresh mint
salt, to taste
pinch of cayenne, optional

PREPARATION

Combine all the ingredients in a bowl and keep chilled until ready to serve. Sprinkle with a pinch of cayenne, if liked.

MIXED FRUIT CHUTNEY

See illustration on pages 130–31.

INGREDIENTS

150ml (¼ pint) cider or fruit vinegar
1 onion, chopped
2 tbsp water
1 tsp ground ginger
zest of ½ orange, chopped
½ tsp salt
pinch of ground cinnamon
1 garlic clove, finely chopped
pinch of crushed, dried, red chilli peppers
125g (4oz) light brown sugar
2 small ripe pears, peeled and diced
1 tart green apple, diced
3 tbsp sultanas, dried cherries or dried cranberries
2 tomatoes, diced
½ Scots bonnet or other hot chilli, chopped

PREPARATION

1 Mix together 125ml (4fl oz) of the vinegar, the onion, water, ginger, orange zest, salt, cinnamon, garlic and crushed chilli peppers in a small pan. Bring to the boil.
2 Add the sugar, pears, apple, sultanas, tomatoes and chopped chilli, then reduce the heat to a slow simmer.
3 Cook until the fruit is soft and the liquid has almost all evaporated. Adjust the sweet-sour balance, adding the remaining vinegar to taste.
4 Leave to cool and serve at room temperature, or pour into sterilized jars while hot and seal. The chutney will keep sealed for up to 1 year.

PINEAPPLE & RED PEPPER CHUTNEY

This relish is delicious with duck, pork or chicken.
See illustration on pages 130–31.

INGREDIENTS

1 pineapple, about 1kg (2lb), peeled, cored and diced
½ red pepper, cored, deseeded and diced
½ lemon, thinly sliced
½ tsp salt
1 tsp ground cinnamon
175g (6oz) Demerara sugar
175g (6oz) white sugar
½ Scots bonnet or other hot red chilli, chopped
¼ tsp ground allspice
3 tbsp white wine vinegar or fruit vinegar
2½ tbsp currants
¼ tsp cumin seeds

PREPARATION

1 Place all the ingredients, except 1 tablespoon of vinegar, in a pan and bring to the boil.
2 Reduce the heat and simmer until the fruit is cooked through and the liquid nearly evaporated.
3 Adjust the sweet-sour balance, adding the remaining vinegar to taste. Leave to cool and serve, or pour hot into sterilized jars and seal. The chutney will keep sealed for up to 1 year.

PICKLED ONION RINGS

See illustration on page 131.

INGREDIENTS

3 large red onions, peeled and sliced crossways
4 tbsp olive oil
6 dried bay leaves, crumbled or ½ tsp herbes de Provence
½ tsp marjoram
pinch of ground allspice
125ml (4fl oz) vinegar
1 garlic clove, finely chopped
1 tbsp dark brown sugar, or to taste
large pinch of cumin seeds
salt, to taste

PREPARATION

1 Separate the onion slices into rings and mix with the other ingredients, turning to coat well. Taste for seasoning, then leave for 1–3 hours at room temperature, or overnight in the refrigerator.
2 Serve the pickle immediately, or spoon into a sterilized jar and seal. It will keep for up to 1 year.

Watercress, Grapefruit,
Orange & Red Pepper
Salad
(see page 135)

Clockwise from top: Salsa (see page 124)
Mixed Fruit Chutney (see page 129)
Pickled Onion Rings (see page 129)
Guacamole (see page 126)
Cucumber-yogurt Relish (see page 129)
Pineapple & Red Pepper Chutney (see page 129)

Middle Eastern
Spiced Pilaff
(see page 133)

Mojo Rojo
(see page 125)

CAMPFIRE BEANS

If short of time, use 1 x 400g (13oz) can of pinto beans, adding more liquid if the mixture seems too thick.

INGREDIENTS

250g (8oz) pinto beans
1 onion, coarsely chopped
125ml (4fl oz) She-devil Barbecue Sauce (see page 127)
1 rasher bacon, optional

PREPARATION

1 Cover the pinto beans with cold water and leave to soak overnight.
2 Drain the beans, return to the pan and cover with fresh water. Bring to the boil, then reduce the heat and simmer for about 2 hours, or until the beans are tender.
3 Combine the beans and their cooking liquid (or the can of beans plus extra liquid) with the onion and the Barbecue Sauce and place in a cooking pan that can withstand the heat of the barbecue. Top with the bacon rasher, if using, then cover.
4 Bake over a cool part of the barbecue for about 1 hour, or long enough for the beans to absorb the smoky scent of the sauce. Remove the lid; if the sauce is thin, return the pan to the barbecue without a cover to let some of the liquid evaporate.

MEDITERRANEAN VEGETABLES WITH SPAGHETTINI

INGREDIENTS

500g (1lb) spaghettini
a selection of Chargrilled Vegetables, such as fennel bulb, red pepper, courgette slices and aubergine slices, cut into bite-sized pieces (see page 10)
3 tbsp olive oil
3 tbsp tomato passata
3 garlic cloves, finely chopped
10 sun-dried tomatoes in oil, drained and diced
handful of fresh basil leaves, coarsely chopped
freshly grated Pecorino or Parmesan

PREPARATION

1 Cook the spaghettini in salted, boiling water until it is al dente, then drain.
2 Meanwhile, heat the chopped barbecued vegetables (and any juices) with the olive oil and tomato passata.
3 Toss the pasta with the vegetables, garlic and sun-dried tomatoes.
4 Serve immediately, sprinkled with the chopped basil and cheese.

REFRIED BEANS

Refried beans, frijoles refritos, *are excellent prepared from dried pinto beans, but if you are short of time, use a 400g (13oz) can of refried beans. Add enough water to give the right consistency (see below) and heat over the barbecue. The beans are a traditional accompaniment with Fajitas (see illustration on page 26).*

INGREDIENTS

400g (13oz) cooked pinto beans (see steps 1-2 left), plus about 125ml (4fl oz) of the cooking liquid
4 tbsp vegetable oil
1 onion, finely chopped
salt, to taste
¼ tsp ground cumin
large pinch of mild chilli powder
250g (8oz) grated cheese, such as mild Cheddar or Pecorino

PREPARATION

1 Mash the cooked pinto beans into the cooking liquid with a potato masher, leaving about a third of the beans whole or partially whole to give a chunky-textured purée.
2 Heat the oil in a large pan, add the chopped onion and sauté until softened. Add salt to taste, sprinkle with the cumin and chilli powder, then add about 125ml (4fl oz) of the bean mixture.
3 Cook over a high heat until the mixture thickens and reduces in volume, then add more puréed beans, stirring and mashing as you cook.
4 When all the beans have been added and the mixture has formed a thick purée about the consistency of fromage frais, it is ready.
5 Sprinkle the bean purée with the cheese and heat until the cheese melts. (Do this on the barbecue for an extra smoky scent.)

BARBECUED VEGETABLE TORTILLA SOUP

Add extra vegetables to the barbecue while cooking, and make this soup the following day.

INGREDIENTS

1 onion, chopped
4–5 garlic cloves, finely chopped
1 tbsp olive oil
½ tsp ground cumin
½ tsp mild chilli powder
½ tsp paprika
250g (8oz) diced tomatoes, fresh or canned
1 litre (1¾ pints) stock
a selection of Chargrilled Vegetables (see page 10),
cut into bite-sized pieces
¼ tsp dried oregano
salt and black pepper
Tabasco, or other hot chilli sauce, to taste
300g (10oz) white cheese, such as
Wensleydale or Pecorino, sliced
1 tbsp chopped fresh coriander
juice of 1 lime
4 big handfuls tortilla chips

PREPARATION

1 Lightly sauté the onion and garlic in the olive oil until softened, then sprinkle in the cumin, chilli and paprika and cook a few minutes longer.
2 Add the tomatoes, stock and barbecued vegetables, then bring to the boil. Reduce the heat and simmer for about 15 minutes.
3 Season with oregano, salt and pepper, and Tabasco. Then place some cheese in each bowl and ladle the hot soup over. Sprinkle with coriander and lime juice. Serve immediately, topped with a handful of tortilla chips.

MIDDLE EASTERN SPICED PILAFF

See illustration on page 131.

INGREDIENTS

90g (3oz) almonds, slivered or whole
60g (2oz) butter
60g (2oz) spaghetti, broken up
2 onions, thinly sliced lengthways
½ tsp ground cinnamon
¼ tsp ground cumin
250g (8oz) long-grain rice
500ml (16fl oz) hot chicken stock
100g (3½oz) raisins

GARLIC & SPRING ONION MASH

See illustration on page 93.

INGREDIENTS

1.5kg (3lb) potatoes, peeled
250ml (8fl oz) milk
1½ garlic bulbs, separated into cloves but unpeeled
2–3 spring onions, thinly sliced
125g (4oz) butter, or to taste
salt and black pepper

PREPARATION

1 Cook the potatoes in boiling, salted water until they are just tender, then drain.
2 Meanwhile, bring the milk to the boil with the garlic. Reduce the heat and simmer until the garlic is tender, about 20 minutes. Pass the garlic cloves through a sieve. Discard the skins.
3 Mash the potatoes with the milk and garlic. Mix in the spring onions and two-thirds of the butter. Season and serve with the remaining butter on top.

ROASTED VEGETABLES VINAIGRETTE

INGREDIENTS

a selection of Chargrilled Vegetables (see page 10)
Classic Vinaigrette (see page 44)
1 garlic clove, finely chopped
2 shallots or small onions, finely chopped
1 tbsp chopped fresh herbs
salt and black pepper

PREPARATION

Dice the vegetables and toss with the vinaigrette. Add the garlic, shallots and herbs, and season.

PREPARATION

1 Sauté the almonds in 15g (½oz) butter until golden brown. Remove from the pan and drain.
2 Add another 15g (½oz) butter and brown the spaghetti lightly. Remove from the pan and drain.
3 Sauté the onions in another 15g (½oz) butter until soft and golden. Sprinkle with half the cinnamon and cumin. Remove from the pan.
4 Sauté the rice in the remaining butter until golden, about 3–4 minutes. Add the hot stock, raisins and remaining cinnamon and cumin. Cover and cook over a low heat until the rice is half done.
5 Add the spaghetti to the rice, cover and cook until the rice and spaghetti are al dente. Fork in the onions and serve topped with the almonds.

ROSEMARY POLENTA

Polenta, poured on to a flat plate or board, is cut into slabs and cooked over the open fire throughout much of the Balkans and Northern Italy. Serve with sausages, poultry or any hearty meat dish, or top with morsels of prosciutto, cheese and herbs for a tasty snack.

INGREDIENTS

200g (7oz) dried polenta
salt, to taste
2–3 tsp finely chopped fresh rosemary
90ml (3fl oz) melted butter or olive oil, plus butter to grease
freshly grated Parmesan, to taste

PREPARATION

1 Cook the polenta in salted water according to package directions, then stir in the rosemary.
2 Meanwhile, butter a large shallow tin. Pour in the hot polenta and spread it evenly. Leave to cool.
3 Light the barbecue or preheat a gas barbecue.
4 When cool, cut the polenta into diamonds, fingers, rounds or any other shape you like.
5 Brush the polenta pieces with melted butter or olive oil, then cook over hot coals until they are slightly browned with marks from the grill. Sprinkle with Parmesan and serve immediately.

SOUTHEAST ASIAN NOODLE SALAD

See illustration on page 17.

INGREDIENTS

250g (8oz) Chinese rice noodles
soy or fish sauce, to taste
2 tbsp vegetable oil
3 spring onions, thinly sliced
½ cucumber, diced
¼ red pepper, diced
Chinese or other chilli paste, to taste
juice of ½ lime
45g (1½oz) dry-roasted peanuts

PREPARATION

1 Cover the noodles with boiling water and leave to soften for about 5 minutes. Rinse in cold water.
2 Bring a pan of water to the boil and add the softened noodles. Cook until just tender, about 3 minutes. Drain and rinse in cold water.
3 Mix together the soy or fish sauce, vegetable oil, spring onions, cucumber, pepper, chilli paste and lime juice. Toss with the noodles.
4 Serve the noodles sprinkled with the peanuts.

MACARONI SALAD

Serve with a hearty meat dish, such as All-American Ribs (see page 24).

INGREDIENTS

250g (8oz) small pasta, such as conchigliette or tubetti
2 celery stalks, chopped
3 spring onions, thinly sliced
½ red pepper, cored, deseeded and diced
½ onion, chopped
1 tomato, diced
1 tbsp chopped fresh parsley
½ tsp paprika
125g (4oz) mayonnaise
3 tbsp mild French mustard
salt and black pepper

PREPARATION

1 Cook the pasta in boiling salted water until al dente, then drain. Rinse the pasta in cold water and drain well again.
2 Toss the pasta in a bowl with the remaining ingredients. Chill until ready to serve.

CUCUMBER, CARROT, RED CABBAGE & GREEN MANGO SALAD

An ideal accompaniment to spicy oriental dishes, such as Bangkok-style Turkey (see page 87).

INGREDIENTS

½ cucumber, cut into julienne strips
1 carrot, coarsely grated
¼ head of red cabbage, thinly sliced
1 green mango, peeled, stoned and cut into strips
2 spring onions, thinly sliced
1 tbsp chopped fresh coriander
¼–½ green Thai or other hot chilli, or to taste, finely chopped
1 tbsp soy sauce
3 tbsp rice, cider or fruit vinegar
2 tbsp sugar, or to taste
45g (1½oz) dry-roasted peanuts

PREPARATION

1 Mix together the cucumber, carrot, red cabbage, mango, spring onions, coriander and chilli in a salad bowl.
2 Just before serving, mix the soy sauce with the vinegar and sugar.
3 Pour the dressing over the salad and toss well, then sprinkle with the peanuts.

WATERCRESS, GRAPEFRUIT, ORANGE & RED PEPPER SALAD

INGREDIENTS

1 grapefruit, sliced
2 oranges, sliced
1 red pepper, cored and sliced or diced
3 cooked beetroot, diced, optional
1 bunch of watercress
2 tbsp olive oil
1 tbsp raspberry vinegar

PREPARATION

Arrange the fruit, pepper, beetroot, if using, and watercress on a platter, or toss together in a salad bowl. Sprinkle with the olive oil and vinegar and serve immediately.

A PLATE OF GREENS & HERBS

The simplest, freshest accompaniment to almost any barbecued food is a plate of crisp, fresh raw vegetables and herbs. Your choice will determine the accent of the meal. Sprinkle with Classic Vinaigrette (see page 44) if liked.

INGREDIENTS

fresh coriander, dill, spring onions and mint; or fresh tarragon and frisée lettuce leaves; or fresh coriander, mint and green chillies; or mixed green leaves, fresh basil and rosemary; or red peppers, thinly sliced onions, chillies, shredded lettuce and lemon juice; or bean-sprouts, peppers, spring onions, thinly sliced celery and fresh coriander; or parsley, sweet marjoram and a fennel bulb, thinly sliced

*Watercress,
Grapefruit,
Orange & Red
Pepper Salad*

135

MENU PLANNING

Abarbecue can be a feast for a special occasion, with each course cooked on the coals – including dessert; or you may choose to have just one barbecued dish while you prepare the rest indoors.

Barbecues are surprisingly adaptable and it is easy to create outdoor menus for all sorts of events, from Sunday lunch to a children's party or an elegant dinner. They are also perfect for vegetarian meals.

RUSTIC ITALIAN DINNER

Each of these courses is redolent of memorable Italian meals. Grilled artichokes are a Sicilian delicacy, and the flavour of the lamb is enhanced by the fragrant smoke. A handful of figs roasted on the dying embers makes a marvellous dessert.

Artichokes with Tomato-tapenade Vinaigrette (page 56)

•

Italian Breast of Lamb (page 96)

Chargrilled Vegetables (page 10)

Rosemary Polenta (page 134) topped with a zesty Italian tomato sauce and Parmesan cheese

•

Honey-basted Figs with Raspberries & Ice-cream (page 121)

ECLECTIC VEGETARIAN DINNER

There are so many vegetable dishes suitable for the barbecue that the days of planning a meal around meat or poultry are long gone. This menu is bright and inspirational, with a tangy salad to balance the rich flavours.

Halloumi, Tomato & Bay Leaf Kebabs (page 119)

Leeks with Creamy Beetroot Vinaigrette (page 51)

•

Stuffed Aubergines (page 56)

Watercress, Grapefruit, Orange & Red Pepper Salad (page 135)

Tofu Tikka in Tomato-pea Masala (page 59)

•

Curaçao Fruit Kebabs (page 122)

Honey-basted Figs with Raspberries & Ice-cream

Watercress, Grapefruit, Orange & Red Pepper Salad

SUNDAY LUNCH

Sunday lunch is one of the glories of the week, when family and friends can gather for a carefree meal. In the summer, this occasion is a natural for the barbecue because both cook and guests can relax outdoors away from the heat of the kitchen. This menu is decidedly South of the Border, as Sunday lunch is a great tradition in Mexico as well.

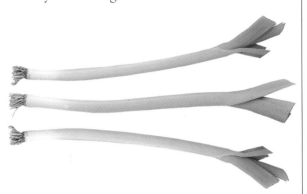

Bruschetta with Tapenade & Rocket (pages 112–13)

———•———

Grilled spring onions or leeks
(see Chargrilled Vegetables, page 10)

Yucatecan Turkey (page 91)

Guava-apple Relish (page 128)

Black Bean Salsa (page 125) with boiled rice

———•———

Zesty Pineapple (page 120)

Yucatecan Turkey

BALKAN & MEDITERRANEAN MIDSUMMER BARBECUE

In Balkan and Mediterranean countries most cooking and eating takes place outdoors all through the summer. A rich cuisine of barbecued foods and flavours has developed, with vegetables and fish being a favourite speciality.

Mediterranean Kebabs (page 59)

———•———

Barbecued courgettes and sliced aubergines, served with olive oil, garlic, parsley and vinegar (see Chargrilled Vegetables, page 10)

Trout Wrapped in Vine Leaves with Bean Sauce (page 61)

Bulgarian Cheese & Onion Flat Bread (page 118)

———•———

Chilled grapes and a selection of cheeses

Trout Wrapped in Vine Leaves with Bean Sauce

FLAVOURS FROM SOUTHEAST ASIA

Southeast Asian cuisine features food cooked over the fire: the smoky scent enhances the spicy hot seasonings to create tastes that are invigorating in the sultry climate.

Malaysian Chilli Prawns (page 74)

———•———

Thai-inspired Pork (page 106)

Southeast Asian Noodle Salad (page 134)

Far Eastern Broccoli (page 53)

———•———

Lush Fruit Feast (page 123)

SPICY SUN-DRENCHED SEAFOOD DINNER

Kebabs of skewered marinated fish and a platter of seafood with spicy mango relish make an enticing sun-splashed menu. Serve chocolate-stuffed bananas for a self-indulgent dessert.

Pasta tossed with Sun-dried Tomato and Basil Butter (page 43)

Fish Kebabs (page 60)

———•———

Seafood with Mango-pepper Relish (page 76) and a salad of al dente green beans, wedges of tomato and Niçoise olives

———•———

Roasted Bananas Stuffed with Chocolate (page 120)

Seafood with Mango-pepper Relish

VERY ELEGANT DINNER

This sophisticated menu is a splendid example of how elegant and stylish barbecued food can be. Serve each course separately and offer ripe fruit for dessert. A rich Italian Stracchino cheese would be a perfect accompaniment.

*Warm Mushroom Salad with
Pine Nuts and Tarragon (page 48)*

Grilled Asparagus (page 50)

Fillet of Beef (page 98)

Chargrilled Radicchio with Gorgonzola (page 49)

Garlic & Spring Onion Mash (page 133)

———•———

A selection of sweet fresh fruit and ripe cheeses

Chargrilled Radicchio with Gorgonzola

OPEN-AIR PARTY FROM THE FRENCH-ITALIAN BORDER

The region of France and Italy that follows the Côte d'Azur and Nice through Monaco, Portofino and Genoa offers some of the most delicious food anywhere. Fresh herbs enhance every dish, especially lamb cooked over a barbecue.

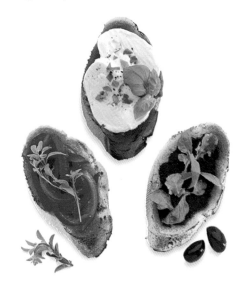

Bruschetta with assorted toppings (pages 112–13)

———•———

Provençal Lamb (page 94)

Sausage Selection (page 111)

Grilled Aubergine Slices (page 51)

A Plate of Greens & Herbs (page 135)

Sausage Selection

MEXICAN FISH BARBECUE

The scent of fish cooked over an open fire at the beach is one of my first memories of Mexico. The spicy pastes coating the fish and seafood are particularly delicious, and the wealth of chilli-based salsas enhances the meal.

Grilled Mussels with Chipotle Salsa (page 77)

•

Smoky-spicy Corn Salad (page 50)

Mayan Swordfish Coated with Annatto & Chilli (page 68)

Chargrilled Vegetables (page 10)

Boiled rice sprinkled with mild chilli powder or ground cumin

Salsa, Roasted Green Chilli Salsa and Black Bean Salsa (pages 124–25)

Mayan Swordfish Coated with Annatto & Chilli

PARTY FOR YOUNG GUESTS

Children love barbecues: there is a holiday atmosphere not found in the kitchen, and they can often prepare part of their own meal. Pizzas are perfect – let the young ones roll out the dough and choose their own toppings. To finish, S'mores are the ideal dessert for the under-12s.

Roasted Carrots (omit the ginger) (page 53)

Barbecued corn-on-the-cob (see Chargrilled Vegetables, page 10)

Barbecued Pizzas (page 114) with additional DIY toppings that children might enjoy: diced ham, bacon, lightly cooked green beans or other vegetables

Finger salad: cucumber spears, raw broccoli, cherry tomatoes, red and yellow peppers

•

S'mores (page 122)

Barbecued pizza

NORTH AFRICAN MENU

Food such as kebabs, fish and aubergines cooked over the fire is the quintessential fare of North Africa, sold in streets and souks. Salads, too, often consist of vegetables cooked over coals, spiced with chermoula or other Moroccan dressing.

Moroccan Lamb Brochettes (in small portions) (page 98)

Mediterranean Fish (page 12)

Middle Eastern Spiced Pilaff (page 133)

Aubergine Salata (page 51)

Beetroot with Moroccan Dressing (page 50)

Mixed Fruit Chutney (page 129)

Middle Eastern Spiced Pilaff

CENTRAL AMERICAN FEAST

The flavours of goat's cheese, chillies and sweet onion relish make a marvellous combination for a starter. Serve the Fajitas with soft flour tortillas, so everyone can assemble their own meal.

Stuffed Peppers (page 54)

Red Onion & Raisin Relish (page 128)

Fajitas (page 99)

Guacamole (page 126)

Refried Beans (page 132)

Salsa (page 124)

Stuffed Peppers

EQUIPMENT & TECHNIQUES

Barbecue cooking is the essence of simplicity.
However, having the right equipment to hand helps to
make you better organized and should prevent any
last-minute dashes from kitchen to barbecue.
This section offers advice on choosing barbecues, from
simple disposable trays to covered models that can
slow-cook whole fish, poultry and large joints.
It illustrates the tools and fuels available and explains
how to get the best results from them. There is also a list
of essential ingredients for a well-stocked storecupboard,
and practical step-by-step instructions show how
to prepare a variety of foods for the barbecue.

BARBECUES

A barbecue is simply a grate or grill suspended over a bed of coals. Cooked on this primitive device, food can take on a very distinct character, absorbing the flavours and aromas of the smoke. Originally the most basic means of cooking, barbecues have become very sophisticated and the range available runs from the disposable tray, which just needs a match putting to it, to elaborate covered models capable of cooking a large joint or even a turkey. Gas and electric models are the most convenient, since they allow year-round barbecuing, give the cook absolute control and eliminate worries about getting the charcoal alight.

COVERED KETTLES

From tiny tabletop portables to 60cm (24in) round, free-standing models, these barbecues are available in a wide range of sizes. The round shape of a covered kettle barbecue reflects heat on to all surfaces and thus cooks food evenly. The cover keeps out oxygen, reducing flare-ups caused by fat falling on the fire, and also keeps the smoke inside, intensifying the smoky perfume (a kettle barbecue can also be used as a smoker). Covered kettles are very reliable, and can of course be used open as well as closed.

HOODED BARBECUES

These large, rectangular barbecues have lids and are set on rolling trolleys. Like kettle barbecues, they can be used covered or open. Temperature gauges, dampers to regulate the air flow, movable grates and cooking grills give refined heat control. Extras such as rôtisseries, side shelves and warming racks are also available, making these barbecues a pleasure to cook with.

The covered kettle's rounded metal lid reflects heat all over the cooking area

Lid hooks conveniently on to side

ADVANTAGES OF COVERED KETTLES & HOODED BARBECUES
▶ *Enable long cooking of large cuts of meat and whole birds.*
▶ *Cut down flare-ups.*
▶ *Give an intense smoky flavour.*

Disposable barbecues come ready to light

DISPOSABLE BARBECUES

Cheap and portable, these little pans come filled with their own charcoal and firelighter, ready to use. They are suitable for hamburgers, sausages, chops or vegetables, and are excellent for picnics.

ADVANTAGES OF DISPOSABLE BARBECUES
▶ *Simple and cheap.*
▶ *Ideal for small spaces — even tiny balconies or patios.*

SAFETY PRECAUTIONS

◆ Never, ever squirt petrol or any other lighting fluid directly on the fire. It can flare back in a split second and envelop you in flames. Use liquid starter only *before* the match has been lit.

◆ Store liquid starter in a safe place, not a warm cupboard or the boot of a car.

◆ Keep the barbecue far from the house, dry leaves, or anything that could catch a spark and ignite. Avoid barbecuing in high winds.

◆ If barbecuing on a wooden surface such as a deck, keep the area well-soaked, using a hose or bucket and water; embers can fall out of the barbecue and set the wood alight.

◆ Watch children and pets carefully to make sure they do not bump into the barbecue and turn it over.

◆ Prevent guests, especially children, from crowding round the barbecue.

◆ Do not barbecue indoors unless you have a model designed for this purpose.

◆ Keep your eye on the barbecue at all times: this is essential for safety reasons, but it can also save any food that is cooking. Sometimes, just a momentary flare-up can turn dinner into something that looks more like charcoal.

◆ For the same reason, keep your tools nearby, so that you do not have to keep running back into the house to fetch them.

◆ Use long-handled cooking tools.

◆ Avoid wearing flowing sleeves when barbecuing and keep any loose clothing away from the grill.

◆ Lift a barbecue cover carefully and away from you, to avoid being burned by steam and smoke.

◆ Don't move the barbecue until the fire is out and the coals have cooled.

GAS & ELECTRIC BARBECUES

Heated by gas or an electric coil, these warm up quickly (about 5–10 minutes), are easy to control and don't produce any messy ashes. Gas canisters last a long time, although in winter you should switch from butane to propane gas, which flows quicker in cold weather. Electric models are just as convenient, though they must be sited near a power point. Regulating the heat on both models is easy, giving control over the cooking process.

Where year-round barbecuing is part of the culture, as in California, many houses have a barbecue as part of the kitchen equipment. Many of these barbecues use lava rock above the burner. When the cooking juices drip on to the rock it creates an aromatic smoke that flavours the food. Lava rocks are natural heat conductors. If they become too greasy, wash or burn the grease off (see unit instructions).

Basket to hold scented woods or herbs to flavour the smoke.

The heat on a gas barbecue is easy to adjust

CHARCOAL BARBECUES

Open-top barbecues can be small tabletop models or larger, free-standing ones. They are ideal for quick-cooking small items such as sausages or burgers, but for large joints of meat or whole fish you really need a lid. It is possible to improvise a lid using foil, but a covered kettle barbecue is the ideal solution. Fatty foods can cause flare-ups, so keep a spray bottle of water at hand.

HOW TO USE A BARBECUE

Cooking on a barbecue is very straightforward. No matter how sophisticated the model is, barbecuing is no more than cooking over an open fire. The most important factors are the preparation, lighting and maintenance of the fire (see below). It is a good idea to have the food prepared in advance so that once the coals are at the right stage you are ready to start cooking.

PREPARING THE FIRE

Allow about an hour to prepare the fire before you begin cooking as coals need about 45 minutes to heat up. If you underestimate how long it takes to get the coals ready, you end up with the frustrating situation of a group of eager guests gathered hopefully around the barbecue while you fumble with matches and uncooperative coals, mentally working out how quickly the food can be cooked.

For food that requires 45–60 minutes' cooking, make a bed of coals two layers deep. When cooking for longer than 45 minutes, you should add more charcoal, allowing 15 minutes for it to ignite.

LIGHTING THE FIRE

There are a number of ways to ignite a fire.
KINDLING Newspapers make the best kindling. Roll up a sheet tightly into a tube, then twist it to make a stick. Place several of these in the bottom of the fuel grate, then set evenly shaped chunks of wood, dry twigs or sticks on top. Over this arrange coals in a pyramid so that there is some air between them. Light the newspaper and, as the fire grows, add more coals. When the coals are hot, spread them out to make an even bed.
FIRELIGHTERS These are very simple to use: just stack the coals around the firelighters, then light.
FLUID STARTER The most commonly used starter, this leaves a chemical taste on coals unless you let it burn off completely. It is dangerous if used incorrectly. Never squirt starter on to a fire once it is burning. The flames can travel back in a split second and turn you into a human torch. Do not even squirt petrol on to hot coals. Immediately you have lit the coals, put away the starter liquid.
ELECTRIC STARTER This is an oval-shaped heating element attached to a long handle with a cord. Place the unit in the coals and plug into an electrical outlet. The starter turns red hot and sets fire to the surrounding coals. Other coals catch, quickly giving an excellent fire. The drawback is that you need a power source nearby.

FIRE CHIMNEY A perforated metal chimney with a handle, this is easy to use. Remove the cooking grill and place the chimney in the grate. Lay crumpled newspaper in the bottom, then stack coals on top and light the paper. Chimneys usually hold 45–50 coals, which light quickly. When well alight, carefully empty the coals into the grate.

TEMPERATURE REQUIRED

Most coals take about 45 minutes to burn down to the even heat required for cooking. If flames are still licking around the coals, the fire is not yet ready for cooking.

The stages of coals described in the recipes are:
HOT Red and glowing, with occasional flare-ups; the coals will begin to form a light layer of grey ash. You can hold your hand no closer than 15cm (6 in) from the coals for 2–3 seconds. Lean foods that cook quickly, such as chicken breasts or fish fillets, may be placed on the grill at this stage; food to be seared can be placed over hot coals, then moved to a cooler spot on the barbecue to cook through.
MEDIUM-HOT The layer of grey ash is thicker, with a red glow only occasionally visible. You can hold your hand over the cooking grill for about 5 seconds. Suitable for ribs and chicken legs.
COOL The coals have a thick layer of grey ash, virtually no red shows, and the fire will be slower. You should be able to hold your hand over the fire for 7–8 seconds when cooking at this heat, which is suitable for long-cooking foods such as sheets of ribs and other large cuts of meat, whole chickens or other poultry.

KEEPING THE FIRE GOING

Most charcoal burns for 45–60 minutes. For longer cooking times, you need to add more coals. Add a few coals directly to the fire or, for a large fire, heat the new supply of coals separately. A second barbecue is useful for this. Use tongs to transfer the coals.

STOKING UP THE FIRE

Tapping coals with tongs will knock off a little ash and heat up the fire. If the barbecue has vents or a hood, open them to allow air to whip up the fire. Add new coals before you begin cooking, or keep the food to one side and add coals to the other.

COOLING DOWN THE FIRE

Spread out the coals with tongs for a less intense bed of heat. Alternatively, cover the barbecue, if it has a hood, and close any vents by about half.

SHUTTING DOWN THE BARBECUE

After retrieving the last morsel from the grill, start putting the fire out. If you have cooked on an open fire, spray the coals with water. If the barbecue has a lid, cover the cooking top and close down all the vents to shut off the air flow.

Don't throw away unburnt material. You can re-use hardwood charcoal, if thoroughly dried after spraying. Combine old coals with fresh ones, as used material takes longer to light and does not burn as hot as fresh coals.

COOKING ON A BARBECUE

OPEN OR COVERED? When you barbecue with an open cooking top, the coals burn hotter because there is a draught. This method is excellent for small items such as chops or burgers because the higher heat chars the food quickly, sealing in the juices.

Larger items such as whole ribs and chicken quarters benefit from a cover. This reduces the flare-ups that could char the outside, leaving the inside raw and uncooked. Air circulates inside a covered barbecue, cooking the food evenly, much like an oven.

DIRECT COOKING Arrange the food on the grill directly over the heat of the coals. The barbecue can be either left open or covered, depending on the size, thickness and fattiness of the food to be cooked.

INDIRECT (USING A DRIP PAN) This method is best for larger, longer-cooking items. Arrange the hot coals at the sides of the fuel bed, then place a drip pan in the centre. Place the cooking grill over it and set the food on top. Cover, and let the juices drip into the pan to make a sauce. Add water, stock or wine to the drip pan for extra moisture while cooking and for a lighter sauce. Top up every 30 minutes or as required. Skim off the fat before serving.

SEARING This is a good technique for foods that cook quickly and tend to dry out, as it seals in the juices. Oil the grill and place the food over a hot fire with the cover off. Cook for 1–2 minutes each side. Finish cooking over a cooler part of the barbecue, or take the food off the grill and let the coals burn down a little before finishing cooking.

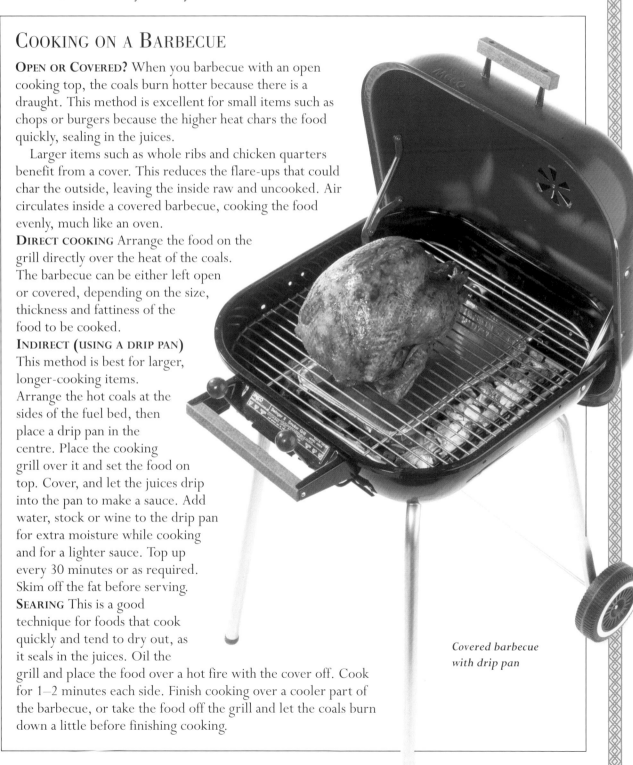

Covered barbecue with drip pan

TOOLS & MATERIALS

As with so many endeavours, having the right tools for the job makes all the difference when barbecuing. Some items, such as forks, tongs and wire baskets, are invaluable for taking food on and off the grill quickly and for turning fragile items without breaking or dropping them. Other tools facilitate basting and glazing.

WIRE BRUSHES
The cooking grill should always be scraped clean with a wire brush after use. Oil the grill before cooking to prevent food sticking to it.

BASTING BRUSHES
Choose a long-handled brush for applying sauces and glazes. You can also make herb and vegetable brushes (see page 152).

SKEWERS
These can be made of wood, bamboo or metal. Soak wooden or bamboo skewers in cold water for about 30 minutes before use to help prevent burning. It is best to use metal skewers for foods that need longer cooking.

MEAT THERMOMETER
Invaluable for testing if large roasts are done.

TONGS
Long-handled tongs enable you to move coals and turn food as it cooks.

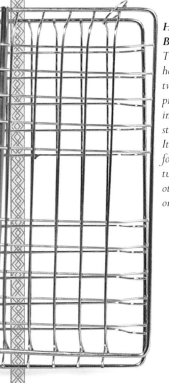

HINGED BASKET
This implement holds food between two wire racks and prevents it slipping into the fire or sticking to the grill. It is very useful for cooking and turning fish and other delicate items or small vegetables.

FORKS
Use a long-handled, double-pronged fork for placing food on the grill or for testing whether vegetables are tender.

SPATULAS
A spatula with a long grip makes it easy to turn delicate foods that fall apart if not handled with care.

FUELS

The basic fuels are briquettes, charcoal and wood chips. Many charcoals such as mesquite and hickory add their own distinctive flavour and scent, and each variety burns at a different speed and heat. Nuts, herbs, spices, seaweed and aromatic woods all make marvellous additions to the smoky scent of the fire, even on gas barbecues. In fact, gas barbecues often have a special compartment designed to hold scented woods or herbs.

BRIQUETTES
Containing wood scraps, sawdust, coal and sand, these are bound together with a petroleum-based substance.

MESQUITE CHARCOAL
Made by the Yaqui Indians in Mexico, this has a woody scent and is clean-burning.

LUMP CHARCOAL
This is made from whole pieces of wood, with no fillers. It burns hotter and cleaner than briquettes.

WOOD
Wood burns more quickly than charcoal. Use chunks of oak, cherry, hickory or maple. Burn until red-hot and lightly covered with grey ash.

TO SCENT THE SMOKE
Wood chips, twigs from fruit trees, vine cuttings, fresh or dried herbs, spices, nuts and seaweed all impart flavour and aroma.

NUTS
Lightly crack almonds, pecans, walnuts, etc., soak for 20 minutes, then toss on the fire.

FRESH OR DRIED HERBS
Place bay leaves, or sprigs of thyme, lavender, rosemary or sage, on the coals or grill. Fennel is classic with fish.

SEAWEED & KELP
To impart the tang of the sea when cooking seafood or fish, add seaweed and kelp to the fire. Store dried, then soak before using.

TWIGS & WOOD CHIPS
Fruit tree and vine cuttings and wood chips can add aroma to the fire. Soak the chips for 30 minutes first.

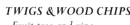

FIREPROOF MITT
Keep several nearby for handling hoods, cooking grills, skewers, spits, drip pans and other hot items.

SPRAY BOTTLE
Filled with water, this should be kept on hand in case of flare-ups.

THE STORECUPBOARD

From soy sauce to chillies, peanut butter to sun-dried tomatoes, storecupboard contents now reflect the global table, so having a good choice to hand will give your barbecues variety and zest. Grow some herbs in pots, if possible, and buy others as needed. Dried herbs and spices are also essential for adding fragrance and character.

FRESH HERBS

I try always to keep a supply of fresh herbs to add their distinctive scents to marinades, flavoured butters and sauces. Basil, coriander, rosemary, thyme, oregano, marjoram, tarragon and mint are all invaluable. Pesto made with fresh basil (see page 124) is excellent in marinades or with simple grilled dishes. Many herbs can be bought growing in pots. Keep them on a windowsill, if possible, and cut as needed. Fresh herbs can also be stored in sealed bags in the refrigerator.

Bay leaves and rosemary twigs can be used to perfume the fire. Place them on the grill or the coals to scent the smoke.

DRIED HERBS

A good supply of dried herbs is extremely useful, especially in the winter when fresh herbs are less readily available. Buy dried herbs in small quantities, store in a cool dark place and check them regularly, as they will eventually lose their savour.

FRESH FLAVOURINGS
Garlic
No other aromatic seasoning goes so well with grilled food. Studded into meats, rubbed on fish, pounded into butters, stirred into marinades, garlic enhances almost anything.
Ginger
This fresh root is available in most supermarkets and should be kept wrapped in clingfilm in the refrigerator. It can be peeled and chopped or it can be grated, in which case it is rarely necessary to peel it first as the skin usually catches in the grater.
Galangal
Galangal is a fresh root, similar to ginger. It has an intense spicy flavour and is an important ingredient in Southeast Asian cooking. Store and prepare as for ginger root.
Lemongrass
Resembling a large spring onion, but smelling and tasting like essence of lemon, lemongrass is increasingly available. Peel off the outer leaves and chop the tender centre stem.

The Onion Family
Finely chopped onions, shallots and spring onions give a subtle flavour to marinades, sauces, savoury butters and relishes.
Lemons, Oranges, Limes
Citrus fruit of all kinds make a fragrant addition to marinades. They can also be squeezed over savoury cooked food and added to salsas and relishes.

DRIED SPICES & FLAVOURINGS
Cumin seeds and powder, cardamom pods, coriander seeds, turmeric, chilli powder and flakes, cayenne pepper, ground ginger, garam masala, paprika, ground cinnamon and cinnamon sticks, peppercorns, star anise and cloves are all essential for rubs and marinades. For spicy marinades and sauces, I suggest using chilli powder or a mixture of chilli powder and paprika if the chilli is too hot. Always use freshly ground black pepper in recipes.

Other useful flavourings are dried garlic and onion granules, especially in dry rubs where

fresh garlic and onion would not combine well with the other dry ingredients.

Annatto Seeds
Available in Southeast Asian shops, these seeds give a spicy flavour and red colour to food. To soften them, cover with water and boil for 5–10 minutes, then leave overnight. The next day cook for 30–45 minutes, until just tender, then purée.

Chipotle Chillies
These extremely hot, dried, smoked chillies have a unique flavour and scent. They add a great smoky flavour – and heat – to barbecue sauce.

Dried Mushrooms
Dried mushrooms such as shiitake, morels, porcini and ceps have a foresty scent that is marvellous with barbecued food. Soak in warm water for 30 minutes, then drain and squeeze dry, saving the liquid for sauces.

BOTTLED & PRESERVED FOODS

Creamed Coconut
This gives a smooth, creamy texture to spicy sauces and can be used to add a Southeast Asian flavour to a variety of dishes. Simply dissolve the creamed coconut in water or use as instructed in the recipe.

Olive Pastes
Both green and black olive pastes (tapenades) bring the scent of the Mediterranean to marinades. They are good spread over simply cooked beef, lamb or fish steaks.

Tamarind Paste
Made from fruit pulp, this acidic flavouring is sold as a paste or in a concentrated block. Tamarind block should be soaked in hot water for 10 minutes, then the juices squeezed out and strained.

Sun-dried Tomatoes
These are available in packets or bottled in oil. Tomatoes in oil are the most practical for barbecuing. If you buy a packet of dried tomatoes, steep them in boiling water until tender, then drain and marinate in olive oil with garlic, vinegar, thyme or herbes de Provence.

Capers
These salty, tangy berries add zest to poultry and fish dishes. Scatter a spoonful over turkey escalopes, or add to a brown butter sauce for skate or other fish.

Syrups
Rich maple syrup and vibrant pomegranate syrup (grenadine) add depth to both sweet and savoury sauces and marinades.

NUTS & DRIED FRUIT

Nuts
The earthy crunch of all kinds of nuts – pine nuts, pistachios, pecans, almonds, cashews and walnuts – is excellent with grilled food. They can be chopped and stirred into marinades or toasted and used for cooked dishes.

Peanuts
Puréed peanuts or peanut butter add richness to Chinese marinades and form the basis of Indonesian Peanut Sauce (see page 124).

Dried Fruit
Raisins, dried apricots and cranberries give a superbly fruity flavour to sweet and savoury relishes and sauces.

OILS, CONDIMENTS & WINES

Oils
Extra-virgin olive oil has the best flavour and aroma; make sure you choose a good-quality one, preferably cold pressed. Hazelnut, walnut and sesame seed oils give a nutty flavour to marinades and sauces.

Hoisin Sauce
A red sweet and spicy purée based on soya beans, this is often used in Chinese-style marinades.

Mustard
Mustard adds punch to sauces, marinades and butters. Keep wholegrain, tarragon, Dijon and herbes de Provence mustards.

Coarse sea salt
Best for texture and flavour.

Soy Sauce
Use dark for "bigger" flavours; light for light meats and fish.

Vinegars
The essential vinegars are fruit vinegars, such as raspberry; wine, cider and balsamic vinegar; and rice vinegar. Flavoured vinegars are also good (see pages 44–45).

Wines
Red and white wine, sherry, port and rice wine tenderize food and flavour marinades and sauces.

PREPARING VEGETABLES

Most vegetables can be barbecued whole or cut into chunks for kebabs. Some, like the aubergine, sweet potato, squash and pumpkin, are excellent slow-cooked, their tender flesh scooped out and mashed for sauces, dips or soups.

Many vegetables benefit from a light marinade; others, such as artichokes and potatoes, are best parboiled. Extra onions, leeks, garlic, chillies and tomatoes cooked on the grill make marvellous ingredients for the following night's supper.

ROASTED GARLIC PUREE

Garlic purée can be added to marinades, flavoured butters, aïoli and soups. Its complex, deep yet mild garlic flavour is magnificent combined with the strong taste and smell of fresh raw garlic. Roasted garlic purée can be kept for up to a week in the refrigerator.

1 Place whole garlic bulbs on the barbecue grill, letting them cook over a slow part of the fire until the flesh is soft and creamy. Separate the cloves.

2 Using a knife, squeeze or scrape out the flesh of the individual cloves. Chop or pound the flesh into a purée, or process in a food processor.

ARTICHOKES

Artichokes must be parboiled before they go on the barbecue. Trim the artichokes, then blanch them in boiling water for 15 minutes. Drain upside-down, then cut in half lengthways and scrape out the inedible "choke" with a teaspoon.

1 Trim the stem and remove the tough lower leaves. Slice off the top and trim the sharp edges of the leaves.

2 Blanch the artichokes, drain and cut in half. Scrape out the hairy "choke" with a small spoon.

BASTING BRUSHES

Celery sticks and leeks, cut into brushes, make excellent mops for basting, as well as adding aroma. Bunches of herbs work well too, tied firmly together.

LEEK BRUSH

Trim the green ends, then slice finely through half its length with a sharp knife.

HERB BRUSH

Tie sprigs of herbs firmly together, then wind string round to make a "handle" and tie securely. Trim the ends.

CHILLIES

VARIETIES There are literally hundreds of varieties of chilli – shown below are some of the most common. Fresh chillies run the gamut from mildly spicy to so hot you want to scream, if only you could find your voice. Generally, the smaller the chilli, the hotter the flavour. Contrary to what many people believe, red chillies are not necessarily hotter than green ones. To prepare, chop or slice thinly. The heat is in the seeds and white pith, so remove these if preferred. Be very careful when handling chillies: always wash your hands afterwards and never touch your face.

TO BARBECUE Chillies of all sizes are marvellous tossed on the barbecue, charred, then peeled. Simply place on the grill, covered to enhance the smoky scent, turning every so often. When evenly but lightly charred, remove and place in a plastic bag or a bowl with a tightly fitting lid. Seal and leave for 30 minutes to steam the skins off. They should then peel easily.

CHILLI FLOWERS

Make lengthways cuts almost to the end of the chilli. Remove the seeds and pith with a knife tip, then leave to open in iced water for 30 minutes. Slivers of green chillies can be used to imitate flower stamens.

Jalapeño or Fresno
Hot green or red Mexican chilli, widely used.

Scots bonnet or Habañero
Very hot, red, yellow or orange chilli.

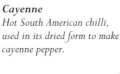

Caribe
Sweet, mild, yellowy-green American chilli.

Birdseye
Tiny, very hot, green or red Asian chilli.

Thai
Hot red or green chilli.

Cayenne
Hot South American chilli, used in its dried form to make cayenne pepper.

Poblano
Mild, dark-green Mexican chilli, known as Ancho in its dried form.

Chipotle
Smoked, dried form of the Jalapeño chilli.

European
Medium-hot, red and green chilli.

Anaheim
Mild, sweet chilli used for grilling and stuffing.

PREPARING SHELLFISH

Shellfish needs only simple preparation, followed by rapid cooking so it doesn't dry out and become tasteless. Make sure the pieces are not so small that they fall through the grill, or use a wire basket to hold them. Squid should be cleaned and then cooked very briefly on the grill before being cut into rings. Lobster and crab can be barbecued ready cooked, absorbing the smoky flavours superbly.

CLEANING SQUID

1 *Hold the squid in one hand and pull the head and tentacles sharply away from the body, drawing out the entrails.*

2 *Cut off the head just above the tentacles. Discard the head and entrails, but reserve the tentacles.*

3 *Rinse out the squid body and remove the long, transparent beak and any remaining innards. Peel off the thin, grey-pink skin and rinse again.*

PREPARING LOBSTER

Lobsters are usually sold ready cooked and need only to be split and cleaned before barbecuing over hot coals.

2 *Pull out the round, white gravel sac near the head and pick out the long thin intestinal vein with a knife. Discard both.*

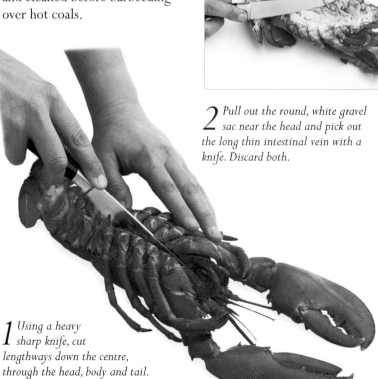

1 *Using a heavy sharp knife, cut lengthways down the centre, through the head, body and tail.*

WRAPPING FISH IN LEAVES

Most fish are delicious when cooked wrapped in leaves (see pages 61 and 67). Fig leaves, vine leaves, citrus leaves and banana leaves all keep food moist and impart their own scent. Vine leaves in brine should be rinsed before use. Banana leaves are available frozen from Chinese and Asian groceries. Defrost, then cut to the size desired. Heat quickly over the barbecue to make them pliable before wrapping. Secure the parcel with fine string, toothpicks or bamboo skewers.

Aluminium foil can be used if leaves are not available, but it does not let in the lovely smoky fragrance.

PREPARING MEAT

Steaks and other small cuts of meat should be of uniform thickness so that they cook evenly and no part becomes dry and listless while the rest is still rare. Spatchcocking, pounding and boning are all techniques that help produce an even thickness. Larger joints of meat, whole poultry and whole large fish, such as salmon, should be cooked slowly, covered, over indirect heat to retain their juices.

SPATCHCOCKING

  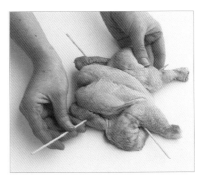

1 Using kitchen scissors, cut through the back of the chicken along both sides of the backbone. Discard the bone.

2 Lay the chicken on a surface, skin-side up, and press down firmly with the heel of your hand to flatten it out.

3 Thread several bamboo skewers to criss-cross through the flesh and hold the chicken flat while it cooks.

POUNDING CHOPS

Pound chops between waxed paper or clingfilm with a wooden mallet. The bones stay attached, forming a handle, while the meat cooks quickly.

BONING A TURKEY THIGH

A boned turkey thigh yields a large "steak" of dark tender meat, perfect for kebabs or for slicing.

1 Remove the skin, if need be, and discard. Using a sharp knife, cut along the muscles that cover the bone. Cut the meat free, scraping to loosen the flesh.

2 Remove the bone and save for making soup. The turkey thigh can be sliced into steaks, medallions or chunks for barbecuing.

BRINING

Brining produces moist, succulent beef or pork with a silky texture.

INGREDIENTS

*125g (4oz) sugar
4 tbsp coarse sea salt
10 each of coriander seeds,
juniper berries, black
peppercorns
5 bay leaves
1 sprig thyme
5 litres (7½ pints) water*

PREPARATION

1 Heat all the ingredients until the sugar and salt dissolve. Cool, then pour over the food to be brined.
2 Leave for 3 days, then rinse the food well and dry. Rub with olive oil before placing on the barbecue.

COOKING TIMES

BEEF

Hamburgers 1.5–2.5cm (¾–1in) thick. Cook over medium-hot coals for 3 minutes on one side. Turn and cook 3 minutes for rare, 5–6 minutes for medium and 10 minutes for well-done.

Steaks Sear for 1 minute per side, then cook for 4–5 minutes per side for rare, 6–7 minutes for medium, 8 minutes for well-done.

Beef or lamb kebabs Cook over medium-hot coals for 3–4 minutes each side for rare, 4–5 minutes for medium.

Rib roast Cook over medium coals, using indirect heat (page 147). For rare, allow 14–16 minutes per 500g (1lb); for medium, 18 minutes per 500g (1lb).

PORK

Loin or rib chops 2.5cm (1in) thick. Sear both sides, then cook, covered, over medium-hot coals for 6–8 minutes per side.

Boneless rolled roast Cook, covered, over medium-hot indirect heat for 25 minutes per 500g (1lb), basting with the drip pan juices until the meat juices run yellow and the internal temperature is 75°C (170°F).

Spare ribs Cook, covered, over medium-hot indirect heat until tender, then directly over the heat to char and darken. Ribs can also be simmered until tender, or precooked in foil, then barbecued over hot coals for 10 minutes per side.

Baby back ribs Cook very slowly over low indirect heat for 1½ hours, or simmer until tender then barbecue quickly over high heat for about 6–8 minutes per side, or until crispy and dark.

Kebabs Cook directly over medium-hot coals, covered or uncovered, for 5–6 minutes per side.

LAMB

Lamb chops 2.5–3.5cm (1–1⅛in) thick. Sear, then cook over medium-hot coals for 4–5 minutes per side for rare, 6–7 minutes for medium.

Butterflied leg of lamb Cook, covered, over medium-hot indirect heat for 15 minutes per side for rare (internal temperature 51°C/125°F), 20 minutes per side for medium (internal temperature 60°C/140°F).

NOTE

Meat thermometers are invaluable for large roasts. For smaller cuts, follow these guidelines: **Rare**: meat will be soft with plenty of give when pressed lightly. **Medium**: meat will yield slightly then bounce back. **Well-done**: meat will be firm.

SAUSAGES

Beef, lamb, pork or veal Prick the skins, then cook over medium-hot coals for about 5 minutes per side. For pork sausages, cook covered for a further 3 minutes per side.

POULTRY

Chicken pieces Sear on both sides over hot coals, then cook over medium-hot coals: dark meat should take about 30 minutes; white meat about 15 minutes.

Chicken breasts, boned Cook over medium-hot coals for 2–3 minutes per side.

Half chicken Sear the skin, then cover and cook over indirect heat or on a cooler part of the grill for about 30 minutes.

Whole chicken Cook, covered, over medium hot, indirect heat for about 1–1½ hours (internal temperature 55°C/135°F).

Wings Cook directly over hot or medium-hot coals for about 10 minutes per side.

Poussins Cook, covered, over medium coals for about 25 minutes.

Turkey breasts Cook cutlets directly over hot coals for 2–3 minutes per side depending on thickness. Cook a whole breast (bone in) over medium-hot indirect heat for about 1 hour.

Turkey thigh steaks or medallions Cook over hot coals for about 2 minutes per side.

Duck breasts Cook over hot coals for about 2 minutes per side, then move to a cooler spot until the meat is pink inside.

Whole duck Remove excess fat then cook, covered, over medium-hot indirect heat for about 1½ hours.

FISH

Whole fish or steaks Cook over hot coals for 10 minutes per 2.5cm (1in) of thickness. Cook whole fish in a wire basket if possible.

Fillets Cook for 2-3 minutes per side, in a wire basket if possible.

Kebabs Cook directly over medium-hot coals for about 5 minutes per side.

Prawns Skewer then cook over hot coals for 3–5 minutes per side.

Clams and mussels Cook, covered, directly over hot coals. Allow 8–10 minutes for mussels, 10–12 minutes for clams, or until they open.

Lobster and crab Cook freshly killed lobsters or crabs directly over hot coals. Allow 12–15 minutes for lobster, 10–12 minutes for crab.

INDEX

Page numbers in **bold** refer to the illustrations.

ACKNOWLEDGMENTS

Author's appreciation
I would like to thank the following people for their help and support. Thank you, Leah, for continuing to eat your way through the recipe testing on the winter holidays from university.
Thanks to my husband Alan McLaughlan for his visits to Berwick Street and Portobello Road markets, laden with shopping bags and wondering what I was going to barbecue next.
Thanks to all those at Dorling Kindersley who have been such a pleasure to work with: Daphne Razazan, who put me in touch with the idea, and Carolyn Ryden, the editor who guided it through to completion; Alexa Stace, project editor and barbecue co-enthusiast, especially when the subject of barbecuing in France came up; art editor Kate Scott.
Thanks to photographer Dave King and the always-hungry Bebe-dog, home economists Nicola Fowler and especially Sunil Vijayakar for his ideas and inspiration.
Thanks to Hoops and Mike Lingwood at Outdoor Chef: kind and generous, they made recipe testing a joy with their gas-fired barbecue. And thank you, Nigel Slater and Richard Cawley, for locating them for me.
To friends in tasting: Jon Harford and his mother Janet, Simon Parkes, Kathleen Griffen, Shirin and the late Michael Simmons, Matthew Robinson, Rhian Parslow, Peter Milne, Jerome Freeman and Sheila Hannon, Esther Novak and John Chendo, Christine and Maureen

Smith, M A Mariner and Richard Careaga, Nigel Patrick and Graham Ketteringham, Amanda Hamilton and Tim Hemmeter, Sandy Waks, Kamala Friedman, Paula Levine, Sheila Dillon, Paul Richardson, Etty and Bruce Blackman (Bruce makes excellent barbecued chicken), Jason Gaber, Helene and Robin Simpson, the Wight family, Georgiana and Harvey Scodel, Fran Irwin and Maria Cianci of the *Chronicle,* Noah and Dinah Stroe, Sue Redgrave, Janice and Derek Gallagher, Vivien Milne and Sue Kreitzman.
To my parents, Caroline and Izzy Smith, Aunt Estelle and Uncle Sy Opper, and grandmother Sophia Dubowsky, who all like a good meal, especially if it's been cooked over the coals.
To Michael Bauer, editor and friend at the *San Francisco Chronicle,* for years of meals, chock-full of camaraderie and gossip, and for commissioning the summer-long series on barbecuing that whetted my appetite for the subject.

Dorling Kindersley would like to thank Nicola Fowler and Sunil Vijayakar for preparing the food that appears throughout the book; Sarah Ponder for the artworks; Julia Schurer of Webers and The Barbecue Shop, Cobham, Surrey, for the loan of barbecues and other equipment; Lorna Damms and Jane Middleton for editorial assistance; and Tracey Clarke for art assistance.